"I hear the tread of pioneers
  Of nations yet to be;
The first low wash of waves where soon
  Shall roll a human sea.

The rudiments of empire here
  Are plastic yet and warm;
The chaos of a mighty world
  Is rounding into form.

—Whittier.

Marula

An imprint of Arcadia Publishing

Pioneer Recollections
Semi-Historic Side Lights on the Early Days of Lansing
by Daniel S. Mevis ("Uncle Dan")

A Marula Historical Reprint
Originally published in 1911

Published by Arcadia Publishing
Charleston SC

ISBN 978-0-7385-9476-7

Printed in the United States of America

For all general information contact Arcadia Publishing at:
Telephone 843-853-2070
Fax 843-853-0044
E-mail sales@arcadiapublishing.com
For customer service and orders:
Toll-Free 1-888-313-2665

Visit us on the Internet at www.arcadiapublishing.com

Pioneer Recollections

Semi-Historic Side Lights
on
The Early Days of Lansing

By Daniel S. Mevis
(Uncle Dan)

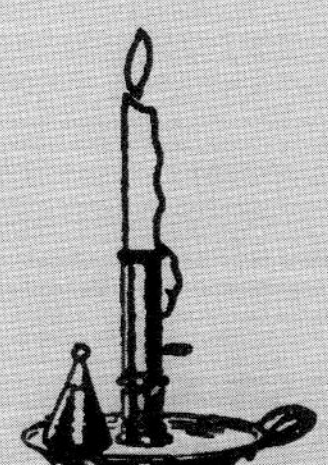

Lansing, Michigan
Robert Smith Printing Company
1911

To

Mrs. Marion M. Turner
the Oldest Living Pioneer and
Earliest Resident of the
Capital City
this book is most
Respectfully Inscribed

INTRODUCTORY.

This little book of "Pioneer Recollections" is published on the urgent solicitation of many friends, it is not intended as a history of Lansing; simply some of the recollections of the author, and dealing for most part with the pre-historic period of the first ten years of the founding and development of the capitol city of the state of Michigan, together with the faces of some of the more prominent pioneers, men who were identified with its life and growth from the felling of the first forest trees to make way for the now beautiful city of which we are all so justly proud.

UNCLE DAN.

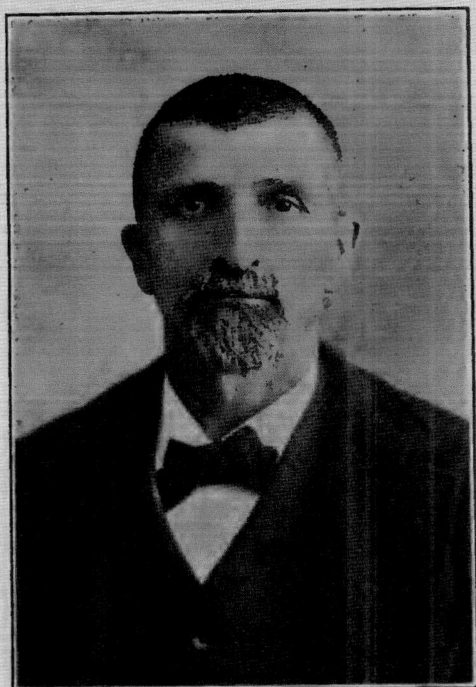

DANIEL S. MEVIS
"Uncle Dan"
1847

STRUGGLES OF BACKWOODSMEN.

A Tale of the Life In Lansing When Wolves Howled Near Doorsteps.

My parents were endowed with a nomadic disposition, so to speak—much of their time being spent on the road. It took but little argument to convince father that there was a better town ahead—accordingly in the summer of 1847, they took the trail to Erie, Pa., but were blown into Buffalo by the greatest storm ever known on Lake Erie.

They boarded the first steamer out, which was bound up the lakes. The captain asked father where we wanted to go.

"Oh, almost anywhere?" was the reply. "Where are you going?"

"To Detroit, and on up," the captain answered.

"All right, we'll go too," and in due time we were landed at Detroit, which appeared to be quite a town.

Start From Detroit.

The household goods all being well packed and in movable condition, it was decided to go on as far as we could get public conveyance. We boarded a car for Pontiac, there being a little railroad between the two towns; while here we first heard of the new capital (to be), "Michigan City," in the interior of the state.

The head of the family soon decided to follow in the wake of the receding capital and accordingly, accompanied by my elder brother, started out through the woods in the direction of the new seat of government. A two days' journey brought the party to a little log grocery, near the North Lansing dam, and being a newcomer and prospective settler, father was soon taken in tow by a long whiskered gentleman, whose business it would seem was to sell lots. After a few preliminary remarks, he frankly asked the old gentleman to "take something." Father took, and the long whiskered gentleman proceeded to elaborate on the great advantages to be obtained by locating at the business center of the new town, claiming, of course, that this dam really settled the question. Factories, mills, etc., would in a short time, be erected the whole length of the mill race, a saw mill being already in active operation.

Again Father "Took Something."

"Take something, uncle." Of course, father took again, and was soon persuaded to buy a lot just as near that dam as possible, but the boy dissuaded his parent from such prompt action, recommending that they look around a little more before deciding. Having heard on the side that there was another town being built farther up the river at the confluence of the Cedar and Grand, they, on the day following, took the trail for "upper town," where Bush, Thomas and Lee were building a city.

They were cordially welcomed by Mr. Thomas, who properly asked father to "take something," which father did. Then Mr. Thomas told the old gentleman how fortunate he was not to buy a lot down at that "end." "Of course, there was the saw mill, but mind you the timber in that locality will all be sawed up in a few years," he said, "and then down goes their dinky little town, while here, you see we are located on high, dry ground and at the juncture of these two great rivers and we will, without doubt, be at the head of navigation, for the Grand river will eventually be dredged from Grand Rapids to this point, giving easy and cheap transportation for the whole Grand river valley and this will be the terminal of a line of river craft, sure to come—sure to come—Take another, stranger?"

Old Man Convinced Again.

It is needless to say father was convinced and thought he wanted a lot as near the mouth of Cedar river as he could get it.

However, the boy again induced his father to withhold his decision until they had investigated the middle ground (later called Middle Town), where the capitol was being erected, but on talking with one or two settlers, learned that there would never be anything doing at this point. Perhaps in time a few residences, and maybe another state building or two.

By this time, in view of the fact that at the end of two short weeks from the time he left Pontiac, mother with the children and two wagon loads of household furniture, would be upon him expecting to find him "settled," and a cabin ready to occupy, the head of the family decided to act without further delay and resolved to buy at once, which he did. He selected a lot at Washington avenue and Saginaw street.

Built a Queer Home.

This he did in order to be near to the mill and

where we would be able to obtain plenty of wood for all time to come, for the mere cutting. Procuring the necessary help, the cabin was built, but none too soon, for at the appointed time the wagons came and we were "at home" at 623 North Washington avenue. After fording the river below the dam we picked our way up the avenue between log heaps and cradle knolls, brush heaps and stumps. The extra sideboards on the wagons served to make the doors and we brought windows with us.

It may be asked how we liked this remarkable change from city life to "a cot in a vast wilderness." Oh, fine, it was not only novel, but really romantic in its way.

Serenaded every night in summer by the denizens of an immense frog pond near the cabin and with clouds of mosquitoes indoors and outdoors adding their plaintive thrills to the grand jubilee of welcome to the "early pioneer"—these and other romantic sights and sounds, such as the snarling of wolves, the distant cry of the panther—like a woman in distress—and watching the pretty deer as they fearlessly browsed among the newly made brush heaps, made for us a new and novel experience.

Had No Firearms.

These deer were perfectly safe, as far as we were concerned, not a gun on the place, and not a man who knew how to shoot one if we had it. I have heard father say that he never shot but one gun in his life, an old musket, when backed up against a brick wall. The wall seemed to stand the shock well—not so with father.

We were, however, frightened later on, when

one evening in early winter the cabin door opened softly and in stalked four big Indians, who, after giving the usual grunt, proceeded to spread their blankets upon the clay earth and lie down, heads to the fire, and remain quietly there until morning. Rising at the first peep of day, they filed out in the same order as they came in, giving us again the grunt. It is needless to say that the only sleeping done in the cabin that night was by those four Indians.

Indians Frequently Called.

We soon found that all our fears were needless as we were frequently visited in like manner, as night would sometimes overtake the Indians when tracking bears. The animals had a long and well-beaten run-way from northern Wisconsin, south to the head of Lake Michigan and then northeasterly, coming through the "Old Maid's" swamp at the head of the Thornapple, and crossing the state road—now Saginaw street—passing through the Chandler, or "Big" marsh, and then north through the Saginaw valley to the straits. They were certainly not in pursuit of deer for they could pick them up almost anywhere in those days. I have seen bears on this same run-way, but never felt like interfering with their progress.

Early Morning Sights.

Father often called us children up in the early morning to look out of the window and see the pretty deer feeding on the tender buds of the recently cut tree tops, while he replenished the fire in the great stone fireplace with its stick and clay chimney—first the big back log; then on great andirons, the "fore stick" or rather log, completing the structure with smaller stuff; then swinging out the "crane" and hanging on the iron tea kettle. This meant breakfast, and we were all soon happy enough when we could breathe in the aroma of bear meat or venison frying in the skillet on the coals. This meat generally bought of the Indians, was cheap, two York shillings or a Spanish quarter buying a saddle of venison or a large piece of bear meat and either was toothsome with our corn cakes and gravy.

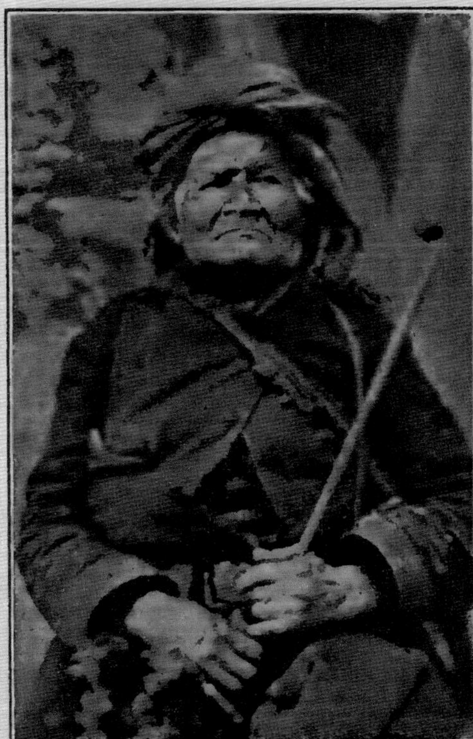

OLD CHIEF OKEMOS

Aged 119 years, the powerful ally of the great Indian Warrior Tecumseh

ROMANCE OF THE REDMAN.

Story of Happy Days Which a White Boy Spent With Okemos Indians.

"I am asked occasionally by some of the rising generation, "Were there any Indians here, Uncle Dan, when you came?"

Oh, yes, there certainly were, but not many, perhaps about one hundred or more, known to the settlers as the Okemos tribe. They resided for some time, we were told, on the Cedar river about seven miles east of Lansing, which would account for the name of Okemos given to that locality. For many years they were in the habit of drifting into town in small parties, disposing of various articles of their handiwork, such as baskets, fancy boxes made of bark, usually of the elm, and decorated with parti-colored porcupine quills; buckskin moccasins decorated with beads and, in their seasons, whortleberries, cranberries, maple sugar, deer skins, fans and occasionally a few wolf heads, on which they obtained a bounty.

Chief Jim Respected.

Their old warrior, Chief Okemos, on account of his advanced age and feebleness of frame, had long since delegated the chieftainship to his youngest son, Jim, who was quite a gentleman. He had been educated in an Indian school and spoke English quite fluently. The eldest son John being a dissolute and all-around bad man, lost his right to the succession. The whites respected Chief Jim highly and his word was of more value than a check on the Macomb County bank. Quiet, genial and good looking, he always seemed to have the affairs of the tribe well in hand. His will was their law, from which there was no appeal.

Though quite a young boy, I became interested in these pre-historic people and soon became acquainted with the boys with whom I later spent many a summer day ranging through the bush; catching black snakes along the river banks and slinging them into the stream; shooting at birds and squirrels with the bow and arrow, and, perhaps, winding up the day's frolic with a swim. I was always a welcome visitor in the camp for many years. The whole tribe were in the habit of camping on the Cooly farm, nearly opposite Waverly park. They camped there for a supply of venison and cured it on the spot.

How Deer Were Caught.

Their method of capturing the deer was not by shooting. They would wait until dark and then start out, two Indians in a canoe, one sitting in the stern and the other on his knees in the bow, where a burning pine knot served for a "Jack light." Armed with a tomahawk and scalping knife, canoe No. 1 would glide noiselessly up the river where the deer would be found standing in the water for protection from the mosquitoes. Mr. deer would gaze intently at the light while the canoe, guided by the man in the stern, who did the paddling, would quietly steal upon him and at the opportune moment, the man on the prow would, with his tomahawk, strike the deer on the head, killing him instantly. This done, the Indians would drop quietly into the water, hip deep probably, and with their knives disembowel the animal and place him in the canoe. This done in less time than it takes to tell it, the Indians would "about face" in the canoe and return to the landing.

Canoe No. 2, in the meantime, was passing up and doing the same thing. Then No. 3 and so on, so that the following morning one could count from three to six deer lying on the bank waiting the attention of the squaws, who proceeded to skin, cut up and cure the venison. The manner of curing was this: A fire was started beside an old rotten log. Wet leaves and moss were raked over it to make a dense smoke; sticks were sharpened and thrust into the ground beside the log and the pieces of meat impaled upon the upper ends over the smudge. In this way the Indians' "staff of life" was made impervious to the fly pest or anything else except the ravenous appetite of the aborigine.

Squaws Prepared Skins.

The skins were treated in much the same way. Tall sticks were driven into the ground and the hides, after the hair had been removed, stretched upon these and a smudge maintained under them until they were thoroughly smoked through and through. They were frequently taken off and rubbed through the hands of the two squaws having the work in charge. I often visited this camp, spending nearly the entire day with Miss Okemos and her elder sister, Mrs. John Turnip, who seemed delighted to entertain the "nechin-we-we—Shemoke-mon"—in their private tepee, where they were sure to be found busily engaged in making fancy articles, such as pretty baskets, and boxes of bark finely decorated with red, white and blue quills of the porcupine; fancy leggings and moccasins, etc. They feasted me on venison and "quash-gon," (bread) and found great sport in teaching me their language.

Escorted Him in Style.

Long before I cared for it, the sun would settle upon the western horizon and Chief Jim would ask me "if I didn't want to go home now?" Of course, I did, that was the proper thing to do. He would whistle and was soon surrounded by half a dozen husky lads all ready to do his bidding. Detailing two to take me home, he would bid me "good-bye and come again," and these young bucks would bring me safely over the rapids.

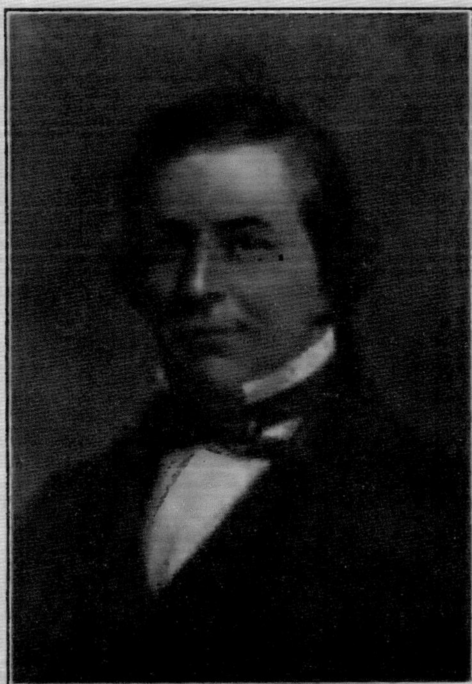

JAMES TURNER
Pioneer business promoter and Real Estate, President
Detroit and Lansing Plank Road Co.
1847

LANSING OF YEARS AGO.

A Spirited Account of the Halcyon Days of the Sturdy Pioneer.

At the close of the Mexican war many of the veterans migrated to the west in quest of government land. A few of these, together with a few veterans of the New York state militia and also of other states, drifted into our little colony, adding to the census of our slowly increasing population the names of many titled heroes—hence we had many colonels, captains, majors and one private, among the notables.

I might mention Col. Joseph Moon, who, when in his cups, claimed the distinction of having fought all through the revolutionary war, and many other wars, and laid much stress on the fact that he was a bosom friend of George Washington; however, the colonel was certainly a great man—when properly stimulated. Of course we had judges, elders, deacons and squires, though captains seemed to predominate.

Everybody Had a Title.

Every man not glorying in a military title was a squire, a few were mere "uncles," but all, or nearly all, were honorable men, having left the east to make for themselves a home in the new west and grow up with the country.

The new capital grew steadily, though slowly, and for a time Upper town outstripped the Dam town and Main street became quite the business avenue with something doing on South Cedar street. Main street had Foot's brick yard at the extreme east end, with Bascom's store next door, and one or two shops on the south side of Main to Cedar, and on the north side was Clapsaddle's hotel (the National), while on the opposite corner was Bush & Thomas' store—all this on the east side of the river.

Pioneer Landmarks.

On the west side was the Michigan house, built and operated by John Thomas, Hunt's meat market, A. Ward's boot and shoe shop, Gilkey's bowling alley, Berry & Co.'s dry goods store, David Westcot's tailor shop, etc., and at Washington avenue and Main street the Benton house was built, the first brick hotel in the city, whose "mine host" for many years was the genial William Hinman, late departed.

The legislature of 1849 directed the state board of auditors to cause a plank walk to be built from this hotel to Franklin avenue, the first real sidewalk of any account built in the city. It was made of two-inch white oak plank, spiked down firmly on oak logs or "sleepers." This was the first tangible event that bound the three towns together into one city with mutual interests. It was with considerable difficulty that members of the legislature, state officers and others could find accommodations, a portion of which was obtained at the lower town and a few at the extreme south end and all, of course, of a very primitive nature.

Political Foes Bunked Together.

The log Lansing house, at Washington avenue and Washtenaw street, near the capitol, was usually taxed to its limited capacity and members of all known political preferments were often obliged to sleep in the same bed and eat at the same table. However, the Whigs being largely in the minority, and the abolitionists much more so, we were rarely startled with any report of a purely political outbreak.

That reminds me of the first political poster I ever saw. It was nailed onto a beech tree, about where the City National bank stands and it read like this:

"Keep it before the people, that 17 old Hunker-orators are about to deluge the county over, but they can't defeat the People's ticket for 1849."

Little Dan was Foxy.

I am reminded also of the first real money I ever captured in my own right. The state built a small dwelling adjoining the capitol for the use of the auditor general (the building is still standing). Deputy Auditor General Peter Wiswold was occupying the house. Mother was to spend the afternoon and evening there and I was to come up in the evening to pilot my mother home. Mrs. Wiswold was "glad I came." She gave me a large piece of real cake, and then a real sixpence, and she said to me thus: "Now, Daniel, my boy, I want you to go to Donahue's saloon and see if Mr. Wiswold is there. If he is, come right back and tell me." I walked into "Donahue's" and very innocently up to "Peter" and looked at him, and he said, "One minute, boys," and then to me, "Dannie, did Mrs. Wiswold send you down to see me?" I nodded my head. He again said, "One minute, boys," and led me out and into the office of the Lansing house, next door, gave me a York shilling and said: "Tell Mrs. Wiswold you saw me at the Lansing house." I again nodded. On my return Mrs. Wiswold gave me another large piece of cake, saying to mother, with fire in her eyes, "Oh, Mrs. Mevis! If he had found him at that Donahue gambling saloon, I'd a gone straight down there; yes, I would—and I'd of picked up a chair and smashed every bottle in the bar and led him out by the ear!"

He Played Both Ends.

Well, right or wrong, "Dannie" was 18 pence to the good, to say nothing of the cake. About this time the state board of auditors were authorized by the legislature to cause all lots or lands belonging to the state on section 16 cleared of its timber. Consequently the board proceeded to let the job, contracting for the same with John Long to clear the S. W. quarter; with J. H. Lobdel the N. W. quarter; with William McGiveron the S. E. quarter and, I think, a Mr. Post the N. E. quarter. Mr. Lobdel built an ashery on a little creek on the east side of Washington avenue, about at the rear end of Shubel's shoe store and utilized the ashes of the entire section and much of the surrounding country in the manufacture of potash, operating his plant for many years. I have caught minnows and pollywogs for "bait" in a little nook of this same creek where the Tussing building now stands.

A "Famous" Rifle.

Fishing in the river afforded great sport as well as a source of food supply, but the hunting did more than this. It gave rival sportsmen opportunity to display their ability in the use of the gun, though it was generally conceded that John Thomas and Charles P. Bush were the two crack shots of the settlement, and Mr. Bush was the proprietor of a telescope rifle. It was once related that at one time when these two nimrods were out together, as they frequently were, they met with a stranger armed with an ordinary smooth-bore. He admired Mr. Bush's rifle and very innocently asked what good was the telescope. Mr. Thomas told him it was a great thing. He could hit a deer with it whether he could see the deer or not, and added that he had a greater gun than that at home, the barrel being circular or crescent shaped, but only took it with him when he went hunting over among the hills.

Pioneers Who Could Shoot.

"With this gun, you see, stranger," he said, "should a deer start up and take round the hill I pull on him and the ball circles on after him and I follow the ball and generally get my deer." They started on and left the stranger in a trance. And then there was John N. Bush, a pretty good shot, but he is still living and can answer for himself. I have heard it said that he would leave a good job on the occasion of a good tracking snow and shoulder his rifle and take to the woods. However, there were many hunters and much game in those days. You could go out in the morning and have venison for dinner.

I frequently indulged in angling in a small way myself, usually just below the dam, where I often found "Ed Grilly," who lived near by and who spent much of his time there and who was a very successful fisherman. He was kind to us boys who gathered there and he often entertained us with remarkable fish stories and gave us good advice at times as to the best methods of angling. He imparted to me at one time a profound secret of the profession. It was this: To procure a small piece of gambogue, put this in your mouth and spit upon the bait. The fish, he claimed, would scent this for a great distance and I would be able to catch all the fish I wanted. I tried the experiment. It did not work on the fish, but it did on me with "immediate effect."

A True Deer Story.

Suffice it to say I lost all confidence in Mr. Grilly. It might occur to some that I have said more about the supply of deer in these articles than the facts would warrant; not so, for they were abundant as any old settler could testify; so plentiful, indeed, that in order to bring a load of marsh hay to town in the winter and land is safely at the stage barns, it often required two men, one to drive the cattle and the other to walk along with a long gad to whip the deer off.

Oh, Those Were the Days.

Well, life was certainly worth the living in those good old days of the early pioneer, when every man knew every other man and all his folks, and where the sentiment of neighborhood fraternity and common interest was the bond that made us, as it were, one great family. If any were sick they were visited; any in want they were assisted; we laughed with those that laughed, and wept with those that wept. Reasonably honest and friendly, the latch string was always out and the helping hand was ever extended to all. Neighbor or stranger, red man or pale-face—we were not proud, for we were all poor.

There were no "styles." That blight happily did not reach the interior for many years. If you were clean and honorable you were a gentleman, though clad in jumper and overalls, and the wife or daughter in their calico or gingham frocks were "dressed" and generally as happy as the "lady" of today. The axe and the indispensable rifle were the only insignia of chivalry and thrift, by the aid of which a man labored to hew out for himself and family a home all their own, happy in the anticipation of a future independence for himself and his posterity, overcoming all hardships and adversities with unselfish, patient endeavor.

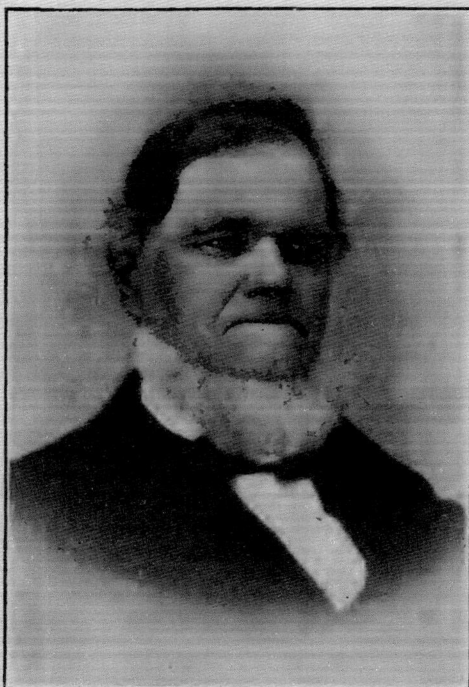

GEO. R. WOODWORTH
Pioneer Boots and Shoes
1854

GETTING LOST IN THE WOODS.

Amusing Pioneer Experience In Which a Cow Is Pressed Into Rescue Service.

The question has been asked me, "Did you ever get lost here in the woods?" Yes, oh yes, but never for any length of time. I always found my way out again. My method was very simple. Many of the settlers owned a cow or two and cows, as well as all other stock, ran at large, and almost any cow of respectibility wore a bell. I would listen for the "tonk" of a bell and go to it. With a gad in one hand I would grasp the bossy's tail firmly in the other and ply the gad. The cow would invariably run for home, guiding me perforce to a clearing.

Once Led Astray.

However, I was once led astray by tying to a strange cow. It was a long run and brought me to a clearing three or four miles away from home. Why on earth my bovine guide did this thing I have never been able to settle in my mind. This was a small clearing with a cabin in the distance. I clambered over the brush fence and made for the cabin. The family—Daniel Barnes, his wife and two children—received me very hospitably and Mrs. Barnes set me up a "snack" which was very acceptible, indeed. I asked Mr. Barnes if that was his cow that I saw over there.

"No," said he, "I have no cow; we don't monkey with any such truck; too much bother. This dog here is the only tame animal I care to keep around. He's a mighty good dog, too, I wouldn't take a farm for him."

I told them I had been lost, but I did not tell them just how I had been led to their home. The old gentleman then told me how to avoid being lost.

"You see, Bub, when you find moss on the butt of a tree you will find it on the north side almost invariably. Just keep in mind which way you start in and you've got all the compass you need. Don't know anybody that wants to buy a little farm like this?"

Is Crowded Out.

"No, uncle, I don't; do you think of selling out?"

"Yes, when I get a chance. You see I've been chased clear from Wayne county to here—moved three or four times. No sooner get settled than neighbors begin to crowd in too close and spoil the hunting and trapping, and break me all up, and now there's a feller got in only a mile west of me, and they're a-building this town four miles east of me (Lansing), and crowding me out again. Game's a-gettin' scarcer every year and so is fur, and that's the main thing with me, but I'll git so far next time they won't catch up with me in a hurry."

And then the kind-hearted gentleman opened the cupboard door and brought out a small brown jug of "ague antidote." I declined.

I told him I was most too young yet to indulge. In fact I was a temperance boy and intended to be a temperance man if I should live to attain my majority. He said that was right. He was a temperance man some of the time, when the "bitters" gave out. He did not go to town very often, "Exceptin' when I get out of ammunition or to get a little flour and things, and then I have to pack them home through the woods on my back."

Mr. Barnes kindly accompanied me to the section line and showed me the way home.

"Follow the blazed trees," says he, "and you'll come out all right."

Coming home I passed by the old forge in "Bogus Swamp" where the surveyors ran upon a trio of men "making money" a year or two previous, not the best kind of money, but fully as good as the wild cat money with which the state was flooded.

In 1849, I think it was, we experienced a local money panic of more than usual severity, though that commodity was always scarce with us. It was on the advent of the first tent show to visit the town. This show was known as "McFarland's Pavilion Theater," hailing from Detroit. They pitched their tent on the corner of Capitol ave. and Washtenaw st. My brother and I erected a lunch stand against the old capitol fence and very fortunately for us we had the only stand on the ground. We had no sooner opened up when my brother "jumped the job"—too much excitement. However, I stayed by until everything was sold. I had drawn on father, who was running a bakery on East Washtenaw st., until his stock was exhausted and then on the pantry at home for all I could get there, and when all the edibles were gone some of the showmen wanted whiskey. Taking an empty root beer bottle I made several trips to Levi Hunt's grocery and bought whiskey. Of course this was the last ditch and business was business. However, with the show and my grocery, it made real money a little scarce for a season.

Invites a Threshing.

Speaking of shows it reminds me very vividly of the year previous. The country was flooded with great posters announcing the advent of a real old time "caravan" over in DeWitt, then the largest town in this section of the country, and for several weeks I lived on the joyful anticipation of seeing that show, and of course I was a remarkably good boy around home, having mother's consent "if father was willing." I interviewed that parent, but alas, too early in the day, and that gentleman informed me that I could not go, therefore, I concluded to go and take the consequences, which undoubtedly meant blue-beech. Well, the long-looked-for day came and as soon as I finished an early breakfast I slipped out of the back door and was soon on the road.

I struck a dog-trot and kept it up until I reined in on the principal street of the then capital city of Clinton county. I was in hopes to be in time to see the parade and certainly would have been had there been a parade. The fact was they had so little to make a free show that they omitted that feature, but this disappointment was soon forgotten. As I headed for the great tent and joined the immense crowd, I was discovered by three "typos" from the office of the Michigan State Journal where I held the position of devil. These gentlemen were O. S. Case, Tate Welch and Henry Starkey. The men seemed to have on their holiday dispositions and hailed me with great hilarity. "Hello, you little cuss, how did you get here? Walk?"

"No, I ran."

"Had any dinner?"

"No."

"Come on," and they guided me up to an extemporized restaurant behind some boxes, roofed with the branches of trees. "Here, captain, give this boy something to eat. Here, Dan, have a pie," says Case, "and this board of ginger bread," says Starkey, while Mr. Welch urged me to take another lemonade, and so they filled me up, giving the "devil more than his due." Then they finished up with me by taking me into the show, and a great show it was, too—an elephant, a cage of monkeys, a cinnamon bear, a coon and a few other such ordinary animals, and a brass band of six pieces, including a bass drum and triangle. But the greater event was yet to come.

Fast Ride to Lansing.

The excitement all over, I started for home. Every rig of any kind in town had been chartered for this trip to DeWitt. Among them was an eccentric old German, Mr. Sagendorf, known as "Old Sag," for short.

Mr. Sagendorf overtook me as I was crossing the bridge and yelled to me to get aboard. "Crawl over the tail board of that wagon quick," he said. As soon as we were off the bridge "Sag" put the bud to the horses.

"Major! Up Tom!" he cried. "Old 'Sag' was the first rig into DeWitt this morning, understand, and he'll be the first one into Lansing tonight, understand. Major! Up Tom!" all this time talking to his trusty blacks. And on we went at a runaway gait over the rough road, passing everything in sight regardless of ruts, holes, logs and stumps. We soon made Hurd's tavern. The landlord ran out to stop the supposed runaway, but "Old Sag" yelled to him to stand clear. On we flew—another team ahead—on went the bud.

"Major! Up Town!"

We passed the team, but to pass "Sag" found it necessary to turn out a little, just enough to run over the end of a log, when down went his load of suffering humanity into the bottom of the wagon, and for the balance of the way we pounded around, so mixed that it was hard to establish our own identity or to escape serious injury among broken glass, fans, parasols, lunch baskets, etc., and then the atmosphere, the aroma of high wines added to the sulphurous stream of profanity and our madman driver's yells to "Major! Up Tom!" made John Gilpin's ride fade away into insignificance. But we were the first rig back, "understand."

Surprise Counterfeiters.

And now a word or two in relation to this gang of counterfeiters who were surprised by the surveyors when running out the "State Road" on the section lines (running west on Saginaw st.), to Allegan, Branch Co., in a swamp, since known as "Bogus Swamp," perhaps a mile west of the city limits. This surveying party came upon three men in a dense thicket busily engaged in coining bogus money—caught them red-handed—the fourth man of the quartet being absent. Of course the gang fled precipitately. The sheriff of Eaton county was notified as soon as it could be done but only one of the party was ever caught. The dies for different denominations of coins were found dexterously secreted in the heels of his boots. The crude forge and a large casting, too ponderous to take with them in their flight, remained for many years on the ground as evidence of their nefarious enterprise. However absurd it might occur to the average law abiding citizen of the present day and generation, I think I am right in saying that in those primitive times counterfeiting and issuing worthless "bank notes" (so-called), was not looked upon as a felony as it would be today. Of course it was taken for granted that it was a "little crooked," but the scarcity of real money, together with the necessity for a medium of exchange, made almost anything that looked like money answer the purpose. As a matter, not only of convenience, but almost of necessity, very much of the business about town was conducted without even the semblance of money, exchanging commodity for commodity, though there were two things that were strictly cash. Those were quinine and taxes. While taxes were very low, the amount of quinine necessary to run the average family for the whole year generally taxed the energy and economy of the head of the family to its utmost. Malaria lurked in every breath of air and poisoned the water you drank. There was no escape and all this from the very nature of existing conditions—heavy timbered land permeated with interminable swamps and marshes, with no other drainage than what they received from the solar system, and not enough of that and the remedy only came when the state wisely passed a general drainage law, one of the most beneficial laws ever put upon the statutes by any legislature since the state was admitted into the union.

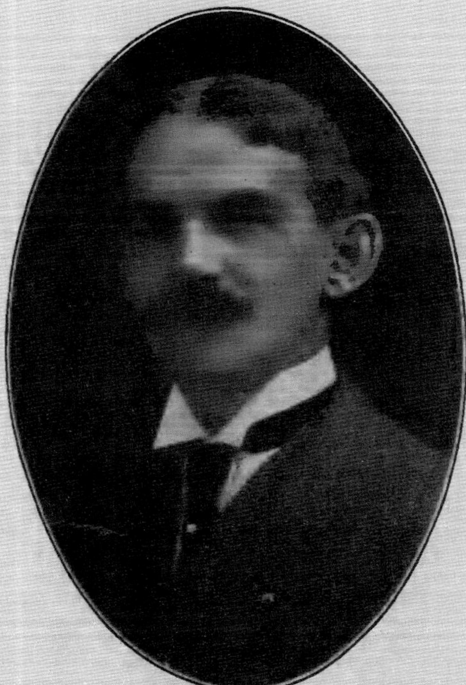

CHRISTIAN BREISCH

Proprietor Pioneer Mills and White Poppy Flour

North Lansing

TALES OF PRIMITIVE DAYS.

Soap Making Is Described—Various Escapades Are Related.

Since "ringing off" my "pioneer articles" I have been importuned by many of the readers of The State Journal to continue the subject; at least to give them one more "story" of those primitive days, confessing that they were very much interested in them indeed. I have yielded, semi-reluctantly, to their desire, inasmuch as I am simply human and easily flattered by the many bouquets that I have received in relation to my former recitals of incidents of early life at the Capital City.

I am convinced that it is not all "soft-soap," for the era of soft-soap making has vanished with the influx of more modern civilization, and general modernism. I no more hear mother say in the early fall:

A Bit of Work for Dannie.

"Now Dannie, my boy, the summer is over, the crops are taken care of, and like a good boy, you have worked hard and faithful and now comes the fall work; soap to make, candles to dip, hogs to kill and your sister to be married. When these are all done the hard work will all be over with again for a long time, and you will have many days to cut up the winter's wood. So tomorrow, you will take the wheelbarrow, the shovel, and the hoe, and go out around where the log heaps have been burned, and scrape up the ashes carefully, and fill the big leach, (a hollow bass-wood log about three feet across and six or seven feet high, on a platform), and we will begin operations at once. It will take all day to get the lye to running. Meanwhile you might take your basket and go up the river and get us a good mess of cowslip greens, that's a good boy."

Thus encouraged I always complied with mother's requests, and only once did it make me any trouble. It was after we had feasted on greens for dinner. Mother sent a portion over to our new neighbors. These neighbors, Mr. and Mrs. John Nelson, were delighted with the herbs, and Mr. Nelson interviewed me on the subject of greens. "What are they? Where do you get them?"

I told him about the nook or cove up the river where they grew in endless quantities. He expressed a determination to go the following Sunday and get a "mess," and wanted me to go with him. But I had to go to Sunday school. He was about to leave me when on second thought he turned and asked:

"Let's see, it's the tops only, that is the leaves, I want, isn't it?"

"Yes, and the roots too," I answered. "The roots are the best part of the greens, very nutritious."

Trouble Is Started.

And here's where the trouble began, I think. On the following morning, Mrs. Nelson came over to see mother and to inquire as to the manner of cooking greens. She said John got them a mess yesterday, and she cooked and cooked them, but it seemed that the roots never would cook tender, and she had thrown them away finally. Just then father came in, and he soon got the whole story. Of course he feared it might make feeling between our new neighbors and us. I managed to keep far enough away from father that he would not step on me for the balance of the day, but the following morning there were "exercises" in the rear of our cabin.

Late in the afternoon Neighbor Nelson met with father as they came out of the woods, and feeling a little sore, probably over the matter, proceeded to call father down for what he termed a downright imposition, for which father was morally responsible, because he had not taught his young ones better manners than playing tricks on innocent strangers. In vain father pleaded that he was not responsible, but when he referred to father as an old hypocrite, then father was touched with deep emotion, and words passed with vindictive fury. Finally a rough and tumble among the underbush followed. Anyway father came home in worse shape than he left us in the morning and from this time on, for many moons, there was a perceptible coolness between the two families. Yes, greens, leeks, berries and wild meat were generally staple components of the early settlers' menu, with a dessert of mush and milk, or maple sugar. Potatoes, of course, were a common commodity, and they would be a luxury now, compared with the poor, sad tubers of today. Yes, even potatoes will degenerate in quality in spite of all the agricultural colleges and modern "improved methods."

A Bit of History.

Well, I think you are expecting a story, albeit let me say, I am not much given to telling stories. Though I do often recite a little unwritten history, which might otherwise be lost to the reading public, I must confess that in this age of fiction a really good and true story might be considered a luxury.

I want to tell the children about my pet canoe, a present from two of old Chief Okemos' grandsons. It looked like a toy boat beside the large regulation canoe. It was of walnut and calculated for a one boy canoe. It was the lightest dug-out I ever saw. The youngsters also instructed me very thoroughly in the Indian mode of handling and propelling a canoe, to skim over the water swiftly, safely and noiselessly, and I can say, without fear of "conflicting evidence" that I became quite an expert canoeist. I could make the course from the foot of Saginaw st. to the Cooley farm in my "little boat" in less time than it takes to tell this story. However, if you believe me, this toy boat of mine got me into more or less trouble. A big boy friend of mine, the late Capt. James Baker, owned a fine, very large canoe of which he was very proud. On a certain bright Sabbath morning he elected to give two young lady friends a ride up the river. It may be you can imagine his displeasure (to use a very mild expression) on arriving at the landing to discover that some one had partly filled his big canoe with water. James was a standpatter and not easily discouraged or turned from his purpose. Accordingly he set hastily to work to bail her out. At about this time I had been seized with a similar disposition to take a sail. However, minus the girls, I dropped down to the river, boarded my little craft, and turned her nose up river and away I went like an arrow, but as noiseless as any redskin.

Baker Falls Out.

I soon sighted James, with his back toward me, and happily unaware of my approach. I glided close to his rear and yelled, "Jim." Of course he was startled, lost his balance and, of course, fell in over "two fathoms of water." For many moons for some reason, James would not speak kindly to me.

Yes, that canoe of mine nearly cost me my life on one occasion. I was starting for the river, thinking to take a little ride. There was nothing selfish about me, hence, I invited an old family friend to go along and have a ride in my canoe. He accepted the invitation and I ran my boat out and seated myself flat on the bottom. I paddled around like a duck for a few minutes in order to show the gentleman how she worked, and then ran ashore and told the friend to get in while I held the canoe steady.

He was somewhat timid about it, but finally stepped in, following my instructions to the letter. He sat flat on the bottom, body straight upright and carefully maintained a perfect equilibrium of the same. I was to push the canoe off when he was ready.

"All ready," says he, "let-er-go."

I did. I gave it a push which sent it to mid stream. Of course, the boat capsized, also our friend, as I had anticipated. Fortunately our friend, William Fitts, was a good swimmer. I was aware of this and watched him with interest as he came puffing and blowing, for the shore, and I saw unmistakable signs of fire in his eyes as he neared the bank. I realized a race through the woods was inevitable and I was on the run none too soon with a man twice my size after me in hot chase. Into the timber I dove at once. I could run like a deer, and did, but my pursuer was handicapped, his Sunday clothes were very wet and his hat, together with one shoe, were yet afloat. However, he gave me a long, hard chase and said some very hard things, indicating what he would do with me if he caught me. All of which made it very desirable for me to keep out of his way, which I easily did. But he reported the matter at my happy home, which made it necessary for me to wait until father had retired before entering the parental abode, and sneaking up to bed. I afterward recovered my canoe, as I had expected to, lodged on the North Lansing boom.

Many Similar Escapades.

With many similar escapades the canoe helped to make life in the wilderness very interesting, indeed, and I seldom overlooked an opportunity to do some new-comer a good turn. And now, while I think of it, I am reminded of a certain Saturday morning, two young men, Henry Kilborne and his brother, armed with rifles, came out of the woods near our cabin. I was out killing snakes. They accosted me asking if there was any game around here. "Oh, yes, some," I replied.

"Well, we're after it," and they started for the timber north of us, when I hailed them asking if they did not wish to shoot a porcupine?

They answered as with one voice, "Sure, where is your porcupine?"

"Oh, just a little way over here," I said.

I led them away for a few blocks to a large

basswood tree, they walked cautiously around and around the tree, peeking up through the branches with guns cocked, ready to fire at the first sight of a porcupine. But failing to discover anything that looked like a porcupine, Henry turned a suspicious look into my innocent face and asked:

"Did you see him go up this tree?"

"Yes, sir," I said.

"When?" he demanded.

"Last Sunday morning," I answered truly.

Of course I was soon lost in the underbrush.

Years after this, if I chanced to meet one of these boys they would look at me with that sharp, penetrating Kilborne look and remark:

"Say, fellers, don't you want to shoot a porcupine? Oh, you little cuss."

Swamp and Many Snakes.

The territory lying along Grand ave., west to the foot of the hill from Ionia st., north to Saginaw st., in those days was a swamp, very wet and fed by springs from under the hill. The swamp was infested with poison sumac, skunk's cabbage, snakes and willows. I once had the hardest snake fight of my life here with a moccasin. Of course, I came off victor. There were striped snakes, green snakes, blue racers, rattlers, black snakes, and during the Civil war, copper-heads. The state caused a deep ditch to be dug along Grand ave. to Saginaw st., and thence to the river, which reclaimed this waste land and made Grand ave. passable in this locality.

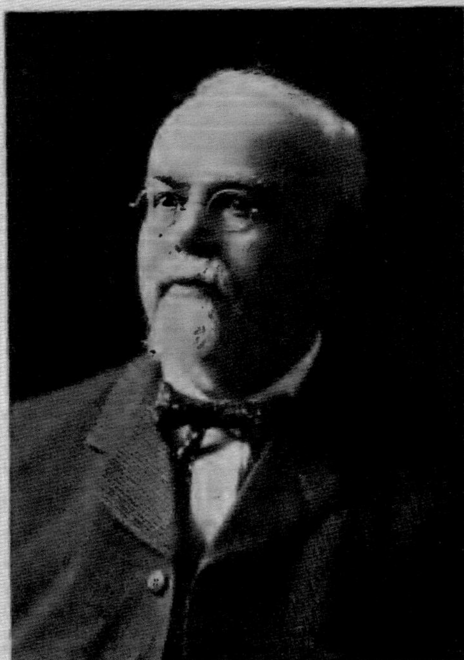

B. F. SIMONS
Pioneer Merchant
1848

VARIOUS KINDS OF SNAKES.

Reptiles of Many Species Were Formerly Found In This Vicinity.

Well, dear public, I am feeling a little sad today. Yes, your poor, old uncle has been suspected of prevaricating. This is as mildly as I can put it, and I would like the floor for a moment while I rise to explain. In my last article I touched incidentally on the subject of "greens." Later on, as I was quietly and peaceably walking down the avenue, I met an old-time friend, who evidently knew but little of pioneer life, who accosted me something like this: "Well, 'Uncle Dan,' I have been quite interested in your articles in The State Journal, and was led to believe you were correct in all you have said, but you were certainly a little off when you went out for greens in the fall. It is in the spring when we get those."

Knows Little of Life in Woods.

Poor man, how little you really know of life in the woods. Did you never read of one John, who lived on locusts and wild honey in the wilderness? Did you never hear of those troublesome people who lived so long on imaginary bread on their march to the promised land? Or poor old Robinson Crusoe, who subsisted so long on a mere island of the sea?

Let me drop a ray of light into the apparent density of my honest friend's cranium, for it strikes me as simply unfortunate that my friend is so utterly unacquainted with the nature and disposition of the festive "cow-slop." It is very evident in my mind that there was something wanting in his "preparatory course." Botany, I dare say, was inadvertently omitted. It is the habit of this particular plant to obtain its development chiefly during the colder months. The foliage and stamens that are gathered in spring for "greens" were put forth and acquired the greater part of their growth the previous autumn, making it possible to collect them late in that season, and are, in fact, more palatable than at any other time. However, the early settlers were not confined to this plant alone for a "mess of greens." We were in the habit of having them all through the summer, from early spring until late fall. The leaves of young basswoods and the aromatic sassafras, the foliage of mustard, which generally flourished "behind the barn," and with which almost any family was supplied, these and many other herbs were generally obtainable if you really wanted them, and we wanted them. Yes, in those days of "nip and tuck," we were likely to want almost anything we could eat, and we could eat almost anything, and a big pot of greens, with its necessary accompaniment, a goodly piece of salt pork, with some good sap vinegar as a condiment, was usually relished by young and old.

No Dandelions Then.

In those early times there were no dandelions, nor dock, in fact but few of the more modern evils that so annoy the husbandman of today.

And while I think of it, let me mention some of the luxuries of the olden times. Hunting wild game for the sport and profit there was in it did not constitute all our pleasures. In late spring and early summer there were wild flowers to gather to decorate the cabin; roots and herbs to collect to be dried and stored away for times of need for the sick; later on, white alder and other berries, and still later cranberries and wild grapes for our fruit supply, and lastly the gathering of nuts to make the long winter evenings about the hearth the more enjoyable. Yes, nothwithstanding all the hard work, those were the happiest days of our life, those days of the boot jack, the great log fire, and the iron crane that swung over it, the old ever-in-use iron tea kettle singing its cheery song, while some were cracking nuts or popping corn, while mother was placidly knitting our winter sox or mending our ragged clothes.

About An Old Man.

Do you see that old gentleman, slowly wending his way through the jostling throng down the avenue, steadying his age-enfeebled step with a buckhorn mounted cane, as he plods his uncertain progress, the gentle breeze playing with his long, white beard, his head thinly crowned with straggling locks made white with the frosts of many winters, his mind absorbed with recollections of a long and strenuous life. And comparing the present with the long ago, he seems almost bewildered. Approach him reverently. Speak to him kindly, and, accommodating your step to his, walk with him, leading him to some convenient seat, sit down, close to him for he is "hard-o'-hearing." He feels lonely. He is fairly hungry for a social chat. Do not allude to his "advanced age." Let him do that. He will tell you of leaving his comfortable home in the east with his young wife and penetrating into the woods. It may be in the immediate vicinity, and locating on "a piece of land," now occupied perhaps by a populous city. He will tell of their first home, the snug cabin, some of the perils and hardships they experienced, their victory over abject poverty, and final independence. The sad part of his story is coming. His children grown to man and womanhood and married left one after another until he and "Hannah" were left to finish the journey of life alone, and then the saddest of all the sad story, and the hardest to tell a stranger. With a deep drawn sigh that convulses his feeble frame, he will tell you of Hannah's demise. His cheeks are wet. They have often been wet before. His eyes lose their faint luster as he affects to look away, with a seeming effort to look through the veil that separates him from his faithful and long wedded wife. Condole with him, and bid him a kind goodbye. Yes, treat the aged kindly, tenderly, for it will not be long.

Something About Snakes.

I think I have not said much about our native snakes. In fact there is such a cloud of uncertainty hanging over this subject that I feel a little nervous myself when called upon to tell a snake story, not but that we had them good and plenty and many species, all kinds and colors, black, blue, gray, green, striped, checkered, ring streaked and speckled. The black snake is essentially a water snake, and though loathsome, is perfectly harmless, generally living along banks of streams. Often the larger ones would be seen stretched at full length upon logs or flood-wood in the sun. The blue racer is strictly a wood snake, and subsists chiefly on small game. The moccasin, one specie of striped snake, the larger green snake and the ring streaked variety infest the swamps. The milk snake is perfectly harmless, but if he finds his way into the cellar, it won't take his lordship long to skim a pan of milk. The copperhead is equally at home on land or water, and is a bad one wherever you find him. The garter or common striped snake, is harmless and of French extraction, I think, judging by his fondness for frogs. The Michigan rattlesnake is another bad one, generally found where he is not appreciated, spending the night on the door step, stretched at full length on a projecting log inside the cabin, or comfortably coiled up under your pillow. The prevailing idea of snake bites is in a degree erroneous. The dreaded rattler does not bite, he strikes with his fangs, which are supplied with tiny sacs of poison. The impact releases the poison which shoots through the inner duct of the fang, and thus is injected into the wound instantaneously. Nearly all the most venomous snakes operate in like manner. The blue racer will bite into your clothing or wherever he can get a good purchase, in order to throw himself around his assailant and about the neck if possible. He will then squeeze with wonderful power. The horned adder, if driven to fight for his life, will, if possible, seize you by the lower extremity of the pants, throw himself around the leg and sting, being armed with a horn or stinger at the end of his tail, and all this with lightning suddenness. This snake is dark blue, and quick as thought in his movements. But do not be frightened, for in all probability you will never get near enough to him to endanger yourself or the snake. The spotted adder is comparatively harmless. The little green or grass snake can be handled for a pet if desirable.

Another Kind of Reptile.

But I would not advise you to do this with his big brother down in the marsh. His manner of warfare is very unique and different from any other member of the serpentine creation. Quickly he may land a mouthful of poisonous phlegm, the color of skim-milk, on the bare skin, and this, according to Indian lore, is more deadly than the dreaded centipede. This reptile is about two feet in length, slim of body, usually found in swamps and located in the thick foliage of the berry bearing shrubs. These were our native snakes. I know but little concerning the reptile population of other countries and climates, but have had an opportunity to become acquainted somewhat with these denizens of the forest. They are generally a bad lot. However, there is this comfort concerning these reptiles. They will, without exception, run from you and endeavor to keep out of your way. You will be perfectly safe, I warrant, if you keep away from them and let them alone.

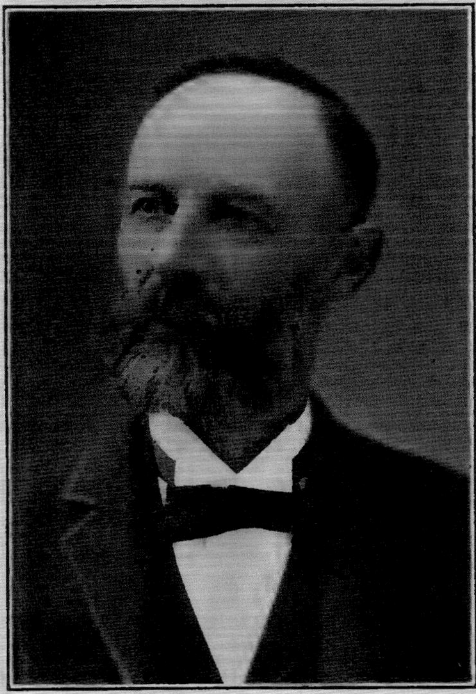

HENRY A. WOODWORTH
Son and successor to Geo. R. Woodworth

OLD PIONEER SETTLERS.

Stories Relative to This Section of State in the Olden Days.

My mother was not a suffragette nor an Amazon, but she was the head of the family all right. Not but what father had the executive ability, when sober, to direct the affairs of our domestic government. Yet I think, from force of habit or otherwise, he did look to mother for advice, for counsel and decision. At all events I know he did do that, for that was the easiest and best way out generally. So while father was looking for some woodman to come and cut the fire wood, mother was inquiring of neighboring settlers where it would be possible to buy a cow, some pigs and chickens, etc., to start us in the little stock raising necessary for self support so far as possible. She found that there lived a widow lady on a farm three miles north of town who would be able to furnish anything she wanted. This was in the spring of 1848. Accordingly mother made a trip to this farm and secured nearly everything desirable, among other things a young porker. On the following morning father took the bed cord from one of the beds and with this my brother and I were sent after the shoat. We found the cabin all right, and the widow, also two tall, gaunt young ladies, dressed in loose gowns, and loose gowns only apparently. The old lady bid the girls to go down with us boys and help catch the best pig in the pen. This pen was the regulation pen, built of logs, squarely in front of the cabin by the roadside, the cabin on a rise of ground about ten rods distant.

"All right," shouted the "girls." "Come on boys," and down the incline they went like deers.

The older girl simply touched the top log of the sty and with one spring cleared it and dropped into the arena. The younger girl less fortunate, and possibly less springy, undertook to do the stunt, but alas, her gown caught on a knot of the log and she lit on her head. Of course it was a terrible shock all round, but fortunately no one was seriously hurt. However, the young lass had no sooner righted herself when her elder sister threw up her hands and yelled out like a locomotive whistle and then at the top of her shrill voice shouted: "Mother, mother, our old sow's dead's a hammer."

And sure enough there lay the poor old mother hog in the embrace of death, and my brother and I both wished fervently that the whole hog family had died also before we reached home with that contrary brute.

I have heard it remarked that we sometimes appreciate our friends most after we have lost them. I think I have a case of this kind in my mind. A friend to rich and poor, and especially to the poor and distressed; a friend, not for the day only, but for a life time verily. For three score years and four, the late lamented Daniel W. Buck exemplified the true and exalted principle of charity in its fullest sense. Being intimately acquainted with Mr. Buck during his long residence here I feel that I am competent to say that during his business career of nearly 65 years he never refused credit to any man, woman or child, especially in the case of burials. I have known many cases of this kind where he never expected to receive a dollar, and he was seldom ever disappointed.

"Well," he would say, "the dead must be buried." And the service was rendered just the same as if he were to get the price, cash in hand. In olden times the undertaker, when notified, with due solemnity, would visit the afflicted family, condole briefly, then proceed to measure the corpse, retire tearfully and return to his factory and set a man to work to make the coffin hurriedly. It might take until far in the night when the receptacle for the body would be completed, trimmed and varnished. Then it would be borne to the house, the shroud put on to the patient object of all these attentions and carefully encoffined. It would then be up to the undertaker, with the kindly assistance of the minister, to conduct the funeral. The undertaker was required to furnish hearse and carriages, all material, time and patience, and all this perhaps with the blessed assurance that he would never realize a dollar for it all. And yet, D. W. Buck uncomplainingly did all this a thousand times, and he was the only man in the business in Lansing that would do it. I feel safe to say that there stands today on the old books of the House of Buck many thousands of dollars that will undoubtedly remain unpaid until the judgment day.

I may be pardoned for this brief mention of my lifelong pioneer friend and erstwhile staunch business man—kind and courteous to all, loved and highly respected by all who had the pleasure of his acquaintance. All honor to the memory of Daniel W. Buck.

My old-time friend, J. N. Bush, told me a good little story on H. Jipson, proprietor of the old Lansing house. It is thus: On one occasion a guest at this hostelry was anxious to get to DeWitt and back that day in order to take the early stage for Detroit next morning. The Portland stage, which ran by way of DeWitt, having been gone for some time, the genial landlord kindly offered to drive him over himself.

The gentleman gladly accepted the courtesy. Accordingly "Jip" hooked onto a buggy and they pulled out for DeWitt. Now there was a very lonely locality on the road at the foot of a hill just where you leave the turnpike to go north on the old road. At this point in that lonely ravine Mr. Jipson stopped his horse, looked very seriously at his stranger guest, and putting his hand to his side coat pocket, remarked: "Well, I think this is as good a time as ever."

The stranger's face blanched. His whole frame trembled, expecting no doubt to see the gleam of a revolver. As Mr. Jipson withdrew his hand there was a gleam, but it was the glimmer of the morning sun, as it came streaming through the tops of the surrounding trees and played upon the glassy surface of a pint bottle. The stranger's rigid face relaxed, the color came back into his pallid cheeks, his eyes lighted up as with a new revelation. He became cheerful and submitted to being "shot in the neck."

I would like to mention a real estate deal of the olden time, brought to my mind from the fact that about every third man we meet now is a real estate agent or his solicitor. There was in the early fifties a Mr. William McGiveron residing on Cedar st., south of Main. This gentleman made a livelihood by furnishing a saw mill on Cedar river in the vicinity with whitewood logs and other valuable timber, and "no questions asked." Mac had about cleaned up on logs within easy access to this mill and was in shape to pull out for new fields of operation and would sell his little four by ten lot home at the first opportunity. The opportunity came one fine morning. Mac discovered a stranger, evidently looking for an opportunity for making an investment. He was very glad to have met Mr. McGiveron, who appeared to be so well informed as to the possibilities and probabilities, the prospects and dead certainties of that very central point of the mighty city of the near future. Suffice it to say that before Mr. Mac let loose of that down-easter, he had sold him forty acres "more or less," for platting purposes, right in the heart of town. Well it was only thirty-nine and three-fourths acres "less."

The "investor" returned to the east immediately, feeling happy over his purchase, and Mr. McGiveron pulled out immediately for the west, also feeling happy.

This reminds me of a grocery order my father "traded out" at one time for "balance on logs" he sold to Mr. M. A. Thayer, the sawyer at North Lansing. The order was on Levi Hunt's grocery for $2.13. These are the items: One gallon whiskey, four pounds sugar (brown, of course), eight pounds codfish, one pound smoking tobacco, one pound loaf sugar, one pound saleratus, one pound sulphur, two pounds Java coffee, one gallon oil, one gallon whiskey, $2.13. Signed M. A. Thayer. Paid, Levi Hunt.

I was dispatched with my hand sled to take the plunder home.

"Be kind to thy father, for now he is old,
His locks intermingle with gray,
His footsteps are feeble, once fearless and bold,
Thy father is passing away.
Be kind to thy father for when thou was't young
Who loved thee as fondly as he,
He caught the first accent that fell from thy tongue
And joined in thy innocent glee.

"Be kind to thy mother, for now on her brow
May traces of sorrow be seen,
Well mayest thou cherish and comfort her now
For loving and kind she has been.
Be kind to thy mother for thee will she pray
As long as God giveth her breath,
For his kind protection, by night and by day.
The love of a mother is stronger than death."

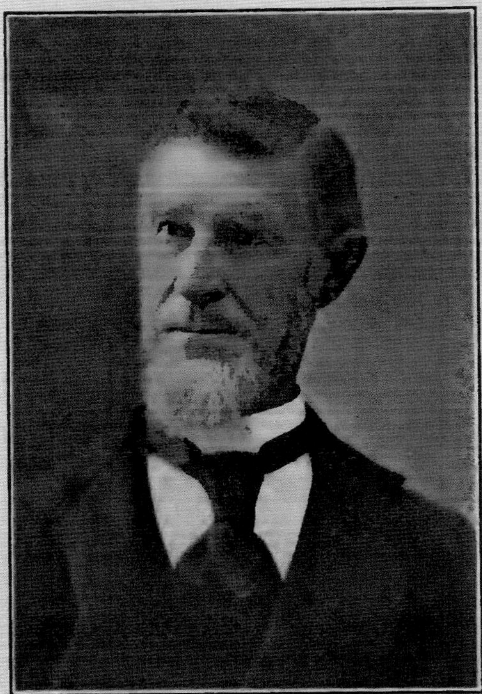

DANIEL W. BUCK
Pioneer Undertaker and Furniture
1847

MICHIGAN'S PRIMITIVE PASTIMES.

Sleigh Rides, Dancing Parties, Corn Husking and Logging Bees.

Considering my three score and nearly fourteen years, I may be pardoned for indulging in a little seeming sentimentality in recalling some incidents of my early life as a pioneer of the Capital City. This circumstance and the fact of having participated as a volunteer soldier in the war of the rebellion, I consider the two greatest events of my life, and in these I feel a conscientious pride. Although I have no regrets as to my experiences as a soldier, yet I am free to admit that I do cherish the memories of my earlier life as a backwoodsman and the son of a pioneer above all other events in my journey from the cradle to the grave, and I love to go back, in my dreamy way, and live it all over again and again; go back and ramble through the woods or wade the rippling brook gathering the luscious cowslip for greens, or the beautiful pond lilies, the queen of the meadow, the moccasin flower, etc., to decorate the mantle shelf, and I fancy at times that I can hear again the singing of the old iron tea-kettle on the great crane in the big fire place and the familiar tick of the old wooden clock in the corner, and again I see my good old busy mother at her daily cares or by the fire light or the light of a tallow "dip," knitting or sewing, mending and darning, and only when I attempt to seize the "snuffers" to snuff the candle for mother do I realize that I am living again in the memory of the days long passed, and awake again to the fact that I am now living in the twentieth century, with its accumulated cares and responsibilities. What wonder that my old heart yearns to go back to the primitive days of my childhood? Not that I really long to be a boy again but for the pleasures of the life in and around the old log cabin in the wilderness, without a care, and few perplexities, as happy as a bird and as free as a young Camanche Indian.

Had Primitive Pastimes.

The old adage was that, "all work and no play make Jack a dull boy," and vice versa, "all play and no work make Jack a lazy boy." In those early days not only Jack, but the whole family were expected to work, yet it was not all work and no play by any means, for young and old, all had their proper seasons for play and enjoyed their primitive pastimes with the true zest born of their very simplicity. There were dancing parties, warm sugar parties, pumpkin peeling parties, corn huskings, logging bees, house raisings and general buzzing bees. Many of these events ended in a round-up at the log tavern for an old fashioned dance, where perhaps the landlord would fiddle and the parson call off.

"And the landlord fiddled hard and long,
While the parson called off good and strong."

And then in winter there were the old time sleigh rides. Often two husky youngsters who boasted the "smartest yoke of steers in the county" would gather up their respective loads and try titles in a friendly race for DeWitt or some other objective point, with, of course, a dance at the terminal. The winter pastimes generally began with Thanksgiving, with its turkey shoot followed by a turkey raffle in the evening. However, the Christmas festivities were generally looked forward to with great interest by young and old as the great event of the social activities, especially so with the children, who counted the days for many moons in anticipation of many things, among which might be plum pudding in lieu of corn mush and sweet cake, and many other delicacies, such as pumpkin pie, dried apple sauce and real "store sugar" for tea and coffee. It was a feast of the soul in the early Christmas eve when the lug-pole was erected in front of the blazing fire place and the stockings were ranged upon it by the expectant little ones, to note the willingness with which they were ready to retire so as not to interrupt or annoy the old gentleman (Santa Claus), should he make an early call.

Swamp Angels.

I can testify to the fact that "Swamp Angels" are not a mere myth any more than are babes in the woods. I have seen both species, and I dare say that almost any old settler, especially if he were a married man and a "fond parent," could vouch for the latter, for we had them, good and plenty. Well, you see, those hardy old pioneers were a very brave as well as a very virtuous race of people, not easily frightened, were not afraid of babies a little bit; I know we were not at our house and there were nine in a bunch, and all nearly of a size. But, now about those angels. I have often seen specimens of these when on my little hunting trips, and found them to be perfectly harmless, though a little shy, generally tall and angular, with very red hair which matches the freckled face and general red appearance of this angelic, bare footed queen of the huckleberry swamp.

Witnesses Marriage.

It was once my unspeakable pleasure to witness the marriage of one of these typical Sirens of the Marsh to a lanky, long-legged, long-haired son of one of the first settlers, at the home of the bride's parents on the confines of the big marsh. Among the many honorable citizens of the town was one George I. Parsons, Esq. I think some of the older citizens will remember that genial limb of the law. Being himself a pioneer and meeting me one Saturday afternoon, he said: "Hello, Dan, just the lad I want to see. Say, do you know where the Fairbanks' place is?"

"Sure," says I

"Well," says his honor, "I have to go there tomorrow to marry a couple, and I would like to have you go along and pilot me out there and then you can witness the certificate. Don't think any of those people can write anyway."

Of course, I was more than willing to go, as I was ever ready to patronize a free show. The squire then told me that "Abe Johnson, the groom-to-be, came to my house very early in the morning, in fact, before I was up, and asked very sheepishly if I would come 'outen' there tomorrow forenoon, saying there were a couple of 'fellers outen there that wanted to git married.' Then he wanted to know if I would wait until fall till he dug his potatoes for my pay, or he would bring me in a load of marsh hay most anytime, as he did not care for the expense. And so, of course, I promised I would. I think we'll get some fun out of it, anyway."

Accordingly we arrived at the cabin about 11 o'clock next day and found everything in readiness for the looked-for event. The bride-to-be was attired in a brand new calico frock, hair combed, face washed, and as smiling—though bashful and shy as a child at a picnic. The groom was attired in a new suit of blue denim overalls and wampus, his cow-hide boots newly greased and both were industriously chewing gum and spooning slyly at each other corner-ways. The old folks looked delighted. In fact, all, including a brother of the bride (Josh), seemed to be full of expectancy and did all that he could to make us feel at home, which we did.

Mother Joins in Smoker.

An "elaborate dinner" had been prepared and was soon spread upon the rude table, and after the ceremony, which was short, we were easily persuaded to have dinner with them. The father of the bride invited us to have a smoke, having provided a supply of pipes and tobacco for the occasion, the old lady joining in the smoker. Meanwhile the newly weds sat as far from us as they could, which was not far, for the room was small and I could easily hear their loving conversation though they talked very low. I heard the groom remark: "I say Jule, you stole something." "Now Abe, what did I steal? I 'aint stole nothing." "Yes, you did; you stole my liver." "Oh, no, Abe, you don't mean your liver, do you? You mean your heart, don't you?" "Heart, Heart? mebby; I know it's one of the big guts."

I indulged in a little conversation with the happy pair in which I asked the bride where she got her gum.

"Over in the spruce swamp," was her buoyant reply, "want some?"

"Sure," says I, and you should have seen with what alacrity that enormous quid of gum came out of her mouth. She bit me off a generous quantity and we took our departure, wishing them much joy, to which they responded, "You're welcome."

Swamps Generally Dry.

Speaking of swamps, there is a very common and indefinite misunderstanding of backwoods lore on this subject, confounding the terms swamp, marsh, swales, cat-hole or any low watery region under the same cognomen. There is a great difference if you stop to consider. A swamp, properly speaking, is generally dry most of the year and more or less wooded, as, for instance, a tamarack swamp, a cedar, spruce or cypress swamp, or it may be a black ash or huckleberry swamp, while a marsh in the strict sense of the word, is not wooded, though in spots it might be pretty wet. Here is where you get your marsh hay. It generally has a dry bottom, and strictly speaking is really a low prairie, and much of this bog is the richest and most valuable land in the state when properly put into condition for cropping.

However, these swamps and marshes were a great help to the early settlers, for they not only furnished good pasture for hogs and cattle through the long summer, but supplied fairly good fodder for winter use. Of course, all stock ran at large, so that often a man seldom saw his hogs until he wanted pork for his table or the barrel. At such times he would shoulder his gun and start for the woods, shooting as many hogs as he thought were his. Returning, he would yoke up the cattle and hook onto a switch and snake home his hogs.

Perhaps some of you young people are puzzled to know what a switch is. Well, it is simply a crotch from a large tree, generally an elm, with a cross bar strongly pinned on and a hole through the noose, through which to pass a log chain, one of the most convenient and, I may say, indispensable implements in clearing up a new farm. With this simple tool for snaking logs out from among the standing timber, the woodsman is well equipped. It is easily made, and of no expense whatever.

Steers Take Fright.

I well remember a little experience with one of these simple contrivances. A friend had elected to gather in his pork crop. I was to assist. Accordingly we shouldered our rifles and waded into the woods to "shoot up." We brought down three sky-cotters and returned and yoked up the cattle and hooked onto the switch and went back after our hogs. We had no sooner succeeded in loading them and securing them properly for transportation on that switch when the cattle took fright and ran pell mell through the woods for home, the switch bounding and rebounding as it went flying through the bush, flying until the frightened steers brought up on either side of a sturdy sapling which brought them to bay. They had turned their yoke here and in order to straighten them out we loosened one ox necessarily, and then there was trouble, for he kicked up his heels and with head up and tail rising he simply made what looked like a moving picture as he swept through the brush on his charge for home. Well, here we were—one ox, one yoke, one switch and three hogs, and one mile from home. However, we succeeded finally in reassembling our outfit and got in all right in time for supper. On my way home I stopped to talk with an old gentleman, a friend of father's, whose son George had left home some weeks previous. I asked the old gentleman where George was now. At this instant the old lady came out and replied to the query, saying, "We got a letter from George day before yesterday and he's in Philimadelphia."

The old gent then asked me, "Where is this Philimadelphia?"

The old lady, with a look of surprise at her lord, says, "Well, I declare for it, Heber, and as old as you are and you don't know where Philimadelphia is. I am ashamed of you, really. Almost any child 10 years old could tell you that."

"Well," says he, "you tell us where it is then if you're so very smart."

"Why, good Lordy, man, don't you know that Philimadelphia is the capitol of the Delawares, to be sure?"

And these people lived within a little more that a stone's throw of a schoolhouse, the "district school," that time-honored institution where so many of the brightest lights in the galaxy of American statesmen have received the inspiration of their lives, lives that are woven indelibly into the life and history of the greatest republic on the face of the earth or anywhere else. What sacred memories cluster around your battered walls and whittled benches!

Pays for "Free Speech."

It was here that I first awoke to the possibilities of the human intellect. It was my good fortune to be something of a favorite with the teacher, who often called me to the platform, not to make an address exactly, but to atone for one I had made in the exercise of the great, and one of the fundamental principles of this government, the right of free speech, or it might be for simply shooting paper wads over at the girls, or having innocently dropped a very crooked pin in the schoolmaster's chair, which had the effect of raising the teacher without raising his salary, and I have often been invited to stop after school for "extra instruction." All these, to say nothing of the puppy loves, the boy scraps and other pastimes incident to the old-time district school.

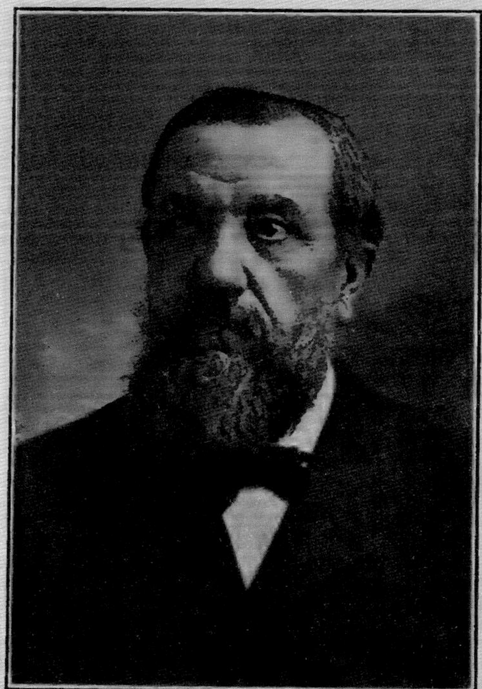

JOHN T. HERRMANN
Pioneer Merchant Tailor

A TALE ABOUT A WITCH.

Story of a Young Man Who Said He Was Turned Into a Horse.

How natural it is when we have reached the sear and yellow epoch of life, and are gliding, softly and almost imperceptibly into our dotage, for the mind to wander back through the vista of the past and to live over again, as it were, many of the pleasant experiences of the long ago. And how much of that past is hallowed by that sacred name "mother." It twines around and permeates the memory of all our youthful joys and sorrows, and forms the keystone of life's architectural structure from the cradle to the grave. But in many ways the mother of the olden time was, it seems to us, somewhat different from the matron of the present day—more domestic, if I may use the term. She looked after her household interests and family affairs in a different way. When the shades of night gathered down in peaceful quiet about the humble cabin, mother always knew where "the children were." They were easily found, undoubtedly gathered in front of the blazing fire, a jolly, happy flock, waiting for mother's call to supper; the meal discussed, the "work done up" and the fun begins. Mother last of all, having put all things to right, seats herself in her accustomed chair, and with "knitting work" in hand, is now at your service, and the "service" is pretty sure to come.

"Now, mother, tell us a story, tell us a witch story or a ghost story, or about the war (1812), when grandfather was a soldier," we would ask, and, of course, mother would gladly grant our clamoring request. I remember a witch story my mother told us one evening.

A Witch Story.

It was a story she had heard her mother tell, when so many good people verily believed in those hobgoblins. The story was like this: On a country road in western New York, there lived an old couple and their only son. This son was a good, steady, industrious boy. For a time he seemed to be going into a decline; his appetite failed him. He became morose and seemed to be weighed down by some great sorrow. It was feared that he was about to be very sick, although he claimed he was not sick. His girl had not gone back on him, or any thing of that kind. Finally, his father demanded an explanation. The boy yielded, and made a clean breast of the whole matter. It was like this: As soon as he was abed and asleep, a witch would enter the chamber through the open window and would, by the proper exercise of her magic wand, turn him into a horse, and ride him away to a distant cemetery. She would tie him to the fence and enter the cemetery, and after spending some time there, return, mount him, and ride him home and with this same wand change him back to his normal condition, though nearly exhausted, and leave him in bed to finish the night. He had been too fearful of consequences to dare to mention it to any one. The old gentleman thought he could see through the whole secret, and said to his son: "Now, John, when she rides you away tonight, you just look sharp to see which way she heads you, and be sure to notice things along the road. Mark the route well, so you will know it by daylight, and at the fence, paw up the ground, gnaw the top board good and plenty so you will recognize it to-morrow. There is a pot of gold buried in that old burying ground, I'll warrant."

The old gentleman was up the following morning long before day, gave Dolly her feed, put a spade or two into the cart and had the rig ready for an early start, nervously anxious for that kettle of gold; therefore. as soon as it was light enough to see their way, while the old lady was putting on a hasty lunch, the head of the family mounted the ladder to call John. But what a sight! What a smell! John was there fast asleep, but such a looking bed, all in a heap, and the headboard was gnawed and splintered beyond recognition. The footboard was kicked completely out and lay on the floor in two pieces. Pot of gold? Oh, no.

The supper is over, the hearth-stone swept,
And in the wood fire's glow
The children cluster to hear a tale
Of that time so long ago

When mama's hair was golden brown,
And the warm blood came and went
O'er the face that could scarce been sweeter then
Than now in its rich content.

The face is wrinkled and care-worn now,
And the golden hair is gray,
But the light that shone in the young girl's eyes,
Has never faded away.

And her needles catch the fire light's gleam,
  As in and out they go,
With the clicking music that mama loves
  In shaping the stocking's toe.

And the waiting children love it, too,
  For they know the "Stocking song"
Brings many a tale to mama's mind,
  Which they may hear ere long.

A Story About Ikey.

Speaking of western New York reminds me of my earlier boyhood, before emigrating to Michigan, then known to most eastern people only as a part of the great northwest. Having but a vague idea of its importance, we were living at Cattoraugus, in the county of the same name, and nearly opposite the Widow Partington. This lady lived in a frame house, had a fine lawn, a barn, lots of fruit and all those things. A neighbor of hers kept a lot of silk worms, had a grove of mulberry trees and made a good living selling silk cocoons. Myself and two other kids were over at the Partington home playing with "Ikey." Something was said regarding these silk worms. Ikey couldn't see why that man kept the dirty things, and when informed that these same worms made the silk of commerce, the silk that was worn, Ikey stoutly refused to believe anything of the sort. While we were in the heat of an argument over the matter, the minister stopped to make Ikey's mother a call. Ikey was incredulous and rushed into the house to ask his mother, for nothing short of a verdict from her could settle it with him. So in he banged and up to his parent, who was conversing with the minister: "Well, now Isaac, what is it?"

"Now, now mother, does the silk worms make the silk we use?"

"Oh, yes, my son. The silk worm makes the silk we use," with a look at the minister (which seemed to say, precious child). And the minister stroked little Ikey's hair and said: "Yes, my little man, the silk worm makes the silk we use."

Ikey Bolts in Again.

And now, says his mother: "Go right out again and play with the boys, and don't come in again until I call you. So thoughtless of you to bolt in like that when I was talking, and with the minister, too. You should be ashamed. And now go right out and play with the boys and don't come in until I call you, understand? Well. Ike came out, but we were soon in another argument. Ikey started it this time, claiming impossible things, and we knew it. But when the argument had run high, and Ikey despaired of carrying his assertions, he made another bolt into the house and rushed up to his mother, who, looking at him pretty sharp, said: "Why, my son, here you are again. Didn't I tell you not five minutes ago not to come in again until I called you, interrupting me when I am talking and with the minister, too. You ought to be ashamed. Now what is it? And then get you out and don't come in until I call you, do you hear?" Ikey allowed that he heard. "Well, now, what is it?"

"Well, mother, don't the tape worms make the tape we use and the pin worms?"

Before Ikey could finish his question his mother had him by the ear, and with one hand she yanked

Ikey, while with the other she opened the door and pitching him out, sprawling on the grass, gave him divine notice that if he dared to come in again before she called him she would break his little neck.

Ikey was a good boy, though cross-eyed and hairlipped.

A friend of mine kindly suggests that I read Victor Hugo's "Les Miserables," etc. I never could enjoy reading those old Greek politicians, and do not care to undertake to ape any other man's "style" or expression. I am satisfied with simply relating my recollections of the early day of my own town. And as to the matter of reading, I do but little of that beyond reading my weekly paper, "The Sunday School Visitor," and the old testament. And allow me to say right here, my friend, there are many good stories in that old book. For instance, 'did you ever read the story of a Mr. Balaam and his ass. This Mr. Balaam was a Moabite, a prophet and diviner, a diplomat in short, at the court of King Zipper, and as such thought to make a little money on the side, and more or less notoriety by cussing the Israelites. But the scheme did not work, and he was obliged to go back as he came. Now this treacherous statesman should have been investigated, tried and condemned to be a millionaire. And the high priest of Allah should have mounted the highest minarette of the mosque of Omar, and blowing his stage horn, yell at the seething mob in the streets below: "To hell with Balaam," and "to hell with Balaam's ass."

And then there is that story, all about Mr. Sampson, a celebrated athlete who, among other things, playfully slipped off the gates of Gaza and carried them up a steep hill and rolled them down onto the

Gazaites. He seemed to have it in for the Philistines, too, went out to war against three thousand of those fellows one day. But they stood up like men and let him slay about a thousand of them with the jaw bone of an ass. Wonder somebody didn't pick up a brick and break his head.

And then again, just for a little amusement likely, caught three hundred foxes, and tying tail to tail, two and two, scratched a match and set fire to these same tails, and then sent those foxes pell-mell through the wheat fields of the Philistines. No wonder that men cry out, "The Philippines be upon you, Uncle Sam." Yes, this is an interesting publication, and I would recommend that a copy be kept in the city library, if it is not there, unless Mr. Baird should object on the grounds that it is to some extent a "work of fiction."

Another Story.

These beautiful October days make me feel quite boyish and bring to mind some of the happy days, a half century back, when with my gun upon my shoulder I traversed the woods adjacent in quest of partridge, quail, turkeys or any other game that came in my way, sometimes getting home with a good full bag and then again with not a thing. I was just thinking of one of these afternoon "rambles," north of town. I came out at a small clearing and beside the road in front of a small new cabin stood an elderly lady who accosted me with: "Say, you ain't a doctor, be you?"

"No," said I. "Not doctor of physics exactly."

"Well," says she, "don't think we want any more o' that exactly, but my ole man's putty sick. Could you just step in and see him?"

"Certainly," said I, and setting my gun down against the cabin, I went in. The old lady leaned over the bed and says: "Lish, here's a man wants to see you."

Lish turned his head toward me and opened his eyes.

I said, "Good afternoon."

He answered me faintly: "Howdy."

The lady says: "You are pretty sick?"

"You bet," answered the patient.

"No fever, no diarrhea?" I ventured.

"Wal no, guess not; you see, stranger, I've been kinder coming down for about two weeks, gitten woss all the time."

"Are you taking anything for it?" I asked.

"Yes, day before yesterday the ole woman sent to town by a neighbor an' got a box o' pills. The readin' on 'em said take from three to five at a dose. Wal, I tuck six so as to be sure, but they made me a darn site worse. However, I meant to give 'em a fair trial, an' last night I tuck six more, an', stranger, I don't think I ever was so sick in all my life es I hev been ever since I tuck them cussed pills. And I want to tell you right here and now, stranger, they don't git no more o' them patent drug store truck down me any more."

Poor man, he was to be pitied. I made no recommendation.

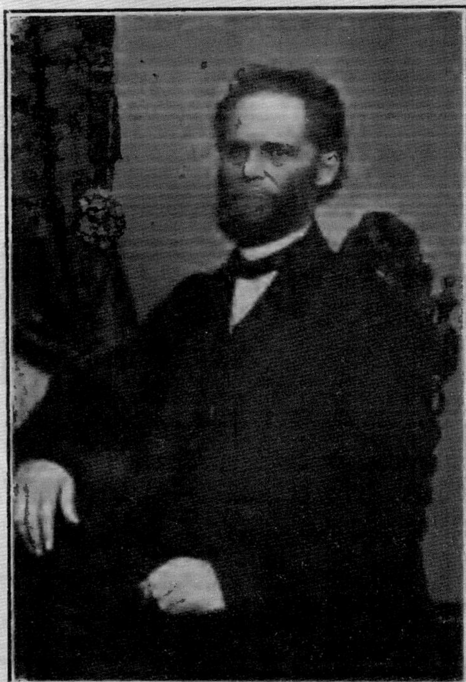

HON. JOHN W. LONGYEAR
M. C., Pioneer Jurist, U. S. Judge Eastern
District Michigan
1849

EARLY HISTORY OF CITY.

Story About a Deacon Who Manufactured Fanning Mills.

Being an old resident and a man of varied experience, my opinion is not unfrequently consulted in regard to the weather. Past, present and future, of course, this subject concerning the weather, I apprehend, has been a mooted question, since the fall of man, and still continues to be the first and leading question, and in all probability will continue to be the same old chestnut while man is permitted to trouble the face of the earth. Of course, we have with us the government weather bureau, which is, as far as it goes, enough for ordinary purposes, but altogether too indefinite, giving us so much doubtful and unsettled atmospheric conditions.

I prefer the old-fashioned, home-made lunar prognosticatory methods of our forefathers, for we must admit that nearly all changes of the weather are preceded by a change of the moon, and vice versa, hence there can be little or no room for doubt or disappointment, and again it is as easy to determine to a certainty at this season or earlier, as to whether the coming winter will be an "open winter" or a stunner, simply by consulting almost any old white haired pioneer who is acquainted with the lay of the land and who has studied the conditions of the muskrat's house or the comparative thickness or thinness of the corn husk as it would be to determine the facts as to the origin of the human family.

Speaking of astronomy reminds me of a little story that the genial and sometimes humorous Dr. H. B. Shank was in the habit of telling to illustrate the "sublime to the ridiculous" proposition. The scene was laid in the state of Missouri. A certain professional pedagogue hailing from one of the northern states ventured down into that country of corn and pork, ostensibly for employment at his profession and incidentally to seek his fortune. He found both, for in less than 90 days he married the oldest and prettiest girl in school, whose father was a rich farmer. The professor was certainly in luck, though the young lady was strictly southern and "native to the soil."

One beautiful moonlight evening, just a year to a day from the event of their marriage, they were sitting on the veranda of the bride-elect's happy home. The professor was contemplating with rapt enthusiasm the gorgeous splendor of the starry heavens. The young and happy bride-elect was chewing gum. Rallying from her apparent stupor she threw an arm around the professor's starchy neck and broke in upon his reverie thus:

"Say, Joe! Joe!"

"Well, my birdling," said Joe.

"Do you remember just a year ago tonight, when we were a settin' right here, as we are now, how you told me how you liked me, and all that? I do my love? I remember well, how well. Say, Joe, how is it by this time? Do you like me as good as you did then?"

"Oh, idol of my heart, I love thee—yes."

"But, say, see here, Joe. I want to hear you

swear to it. You know dad won't believe anybody lest they swear to it."

"Yes, my love, my life, I swear by yon effulgent moon."

"Hold on, Joe, not by the moon. For you know the moon changes. Anyhow they say it does."

"Well, my precious heart, I swear by yon twinkling stars."

"Oh, come off, Joe. Git down to solid earth onc't."

"Then, my love, my queen, tell me of some great power whereby I shall pledge my undying love and devotion."

"I'll tell ye, Joe. You swear by the pork crop, dad says that never fails."

There came a time when Dr. R. J. Shank was nominated for alderman for the Second ward by the Democrats. Accordingly the Republicans proceeded to nominate R. B. Shank, the doctor's brother, for the same office. On the morning of election the old doctor, father of this pair of Shanks, proceeded to the polls and wrote upon the back of his ticket, "To choose between the pups 'tis a difficult job, but when worst comes to worst, put this in for Bob."

At another time in the city's history, a Mr. Sears, who had established a canning industry, was stricken down by the grim reaper. His widow wrote the doctor for his advice as to her continuing the business. The humorous doctor indorsed upon the back of the letter

"My dear Mrs. Sears. Don't give way to your tears, but fill to the brim every can. The sun and the moon will come round just as soon, and so will some other nice man."

This quaint and popular pioneer and public-spirited practitioner will be remembered by many of the old settlers, as well as by many of the present generation, for the name of Shank was for many years a household word, together with the fact that the elder doctor and his two sons, Rush J. and Robert B., were swept off the city directory by the fell destroyer within so short a time. R. B. Shank's demise was keenly felt by the middle class of consumers on account of his business methods, keeping down the price of the necessities of life, and it was here as a clerk, though but a boy, that F. M. Loftus learned the secret of the successful business tact that has made him so popular, as the successor to R. B. Stank, the pioneer business man.

There is a great deal being said in our day in regard to many of the statutory laws that interfere with the liberties of our undesirable citizens. I will admit that many of our laws are of little good so far as the public weal is concerned, and I would suggest a revision of both the civil and the criminal code. More particularly in the matter of marriages and divorces. I think it would be well to amend the law in relation to the marriage contract, binding the contracting parties under oath to keep the peace for at least a twelvemonth from the time the contract takes effect, and making it obligatory that all marriage services be performed by a magistrate. There is, or seems to be, a crying need for a more stringent law in regard to suicide, something that would make suicide a penal offense. This matter has undoubtedly been overlooked by successive legislatures. I simply throw out these suggestions, hoping that it may meet the all-seeing eye of his excellency, Governor Osborn, that he may perhaps incorporate a recommendation to this effect in his inaugural message to the next legislature.

I want to stop the clock right here while I tell you of an incident in the business career of good, old Deacon John R. Price of the north end. The deacon's business, when he was not preaching or praying, was manufacturing fanning mills. These mills he sold to the settlers on new farms, generally, and in many cases on time, taking notes for a part, or it might be the entire price of the little mill. One of these debtors, whose note was long overdue, and whom he had notified of this fact at different times, in order to satisfy the deacon of his honest intention to square the account, since money was simply out of the question, offered to haul him saw logs to satisfy the account. Barkis was willing.

Now, there was adjacent to this delinquent settler's little estate a fine tract of timber—"non-resident" land. Accordingly, as had been his custom, he waded into this unknown's forest and cut the necessary logs, yoked his cattle, hooked onto his sled and proceeded to haul out as many as was necessary to cover the indebtedness. But woe the day. As he was coming out of the woods the front of the sled struck a small stump and put a sudden stop to further progress. Well, the air soon became a bright blue around that load of logs, and in his extremity, mingled with rage, he caused the cattle to step aside, and stepping in between them and seizing his ax proceeded to cut this offensive little stump as best he could. But alas, the ax glanced and struck an ox's leg just above the foot, making it necessary to slaughter the ox. Well, the logs were finally delivered at the mill and the unfortunate man in settling with the deacon, told him the story of his misfortune, adding: "So you see, deacon, it was through me honesty and me uprightness that I lost me ox."

God save the mark; stealing timber to pay an honest debt. But how many there are that do that.

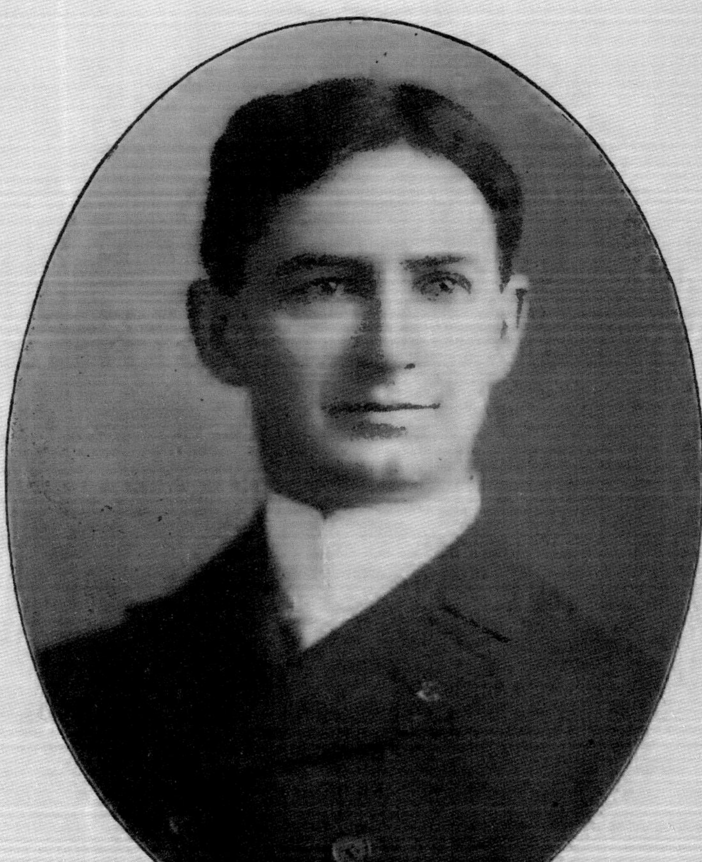

F. M. LOFTUS
Successor to Pioneer Grocery

PRESBYTERIAN SUNDAY SCHOOL.

Account of the Organization of the Church Society in City.

Early in the spring of 1847 Joshua French erected a block house on East Washtenaw street (about 119). This was one of the better class of log houses, the logs being hewn outside and inside. The house had a shingled roof, a staircase, in lieu of the usual ladder, partitions of matched lumber, a paneled front door and eight by ten glass in each of the windows in lieu of the more ordinary seven by nines. Mr. French's stay was very short, he becoming discouraged on account of mosquitoes, ague and the absence of the conveniences and luxuries of his eastern life. Fortunately having money enough left to make it possible he returned to his York state home. Subsequently Charles T. Allen occupied the house for a few years and later my people lived there for quite a number of years, maintaining a boarding house.

Oven Falls on Father.

My father was a baker, one of ye olden time, and he erected a bakery just west of the house. In connection, of course, he had an oven constructed, a large one, built under his own personal supervision, in order to have it right. However, prematurely, father being anxious to get to doing business, he crawled into the oven to remove the stays from under the arch, and the whole thing, arch and all, came down, nearly crushing father under the brick, sand and grouting that constituted the great arch, and for a short time father was in a tight place sure enough. Mother and I had to work pretty lively for some time to liberate "Hiram." I did not dare to laugh then and there, and really I would not, out of respect to father, he being of a very energetic disposition, and if he should feel it his duty to chastise a boy, or anything like that, it might prove too great a strain for a man of his years, and very early in life I had occasion to realize the force of the ancient seer's remarks when he ventured the opinion that there is a time to laugh and a time to weep.

This reminds me of a little incident of later years. J. C. Bailey was about to build the City National bank building and proposed to get his bearings correct by taking measurements from the monument or quarter post at Michigan and Washington avenues. He cited Mr. Roark, his man of all work, to be at that point next morning. Mr. Roark came, but a little late, and in tears. Mr. Bailey asked him what his trouble was.

"Trouble enough," says Roark.

"Are you crying for grief or for joy, Pat?"

"Indade, it's for both, Mr. Bailey. Oi'm crying for joy to know oi've got a 'bye' that is able to whip his father, but oi'm crying for grief because he did it this very morning, sor."

East Washtenaw street and down River street to Main were quite business streets in those days—Penny Johnson's little grocery, father's bakery and boarding house, the stage barns, Bennett's wagon shop, the Godly's and the Hobs Bros.' blacksmith shops, Alton's cooperage and Yeiters' brewery. There remains a trace of hallowed memory in connection with this old block house. It was here in the winter of 1849 that a little knot of settlers gathered to discuss the feasibility of organizing a Presbyterian church society, meeting with the family of Charles T. Allen. Here was organized the first Presbyterian Sunday school. I was a charter member.

Uncle Dan City Crier.

I think I will step down now into a more recent generation, just in order to mention the fact that I, myself, was once a city officer. On the occasion of the first meeting of the first city council I was elected or appointed, as the case might be, as city crier. Now, aside from its being one of the appointive offices, authorized by the charter, it was no mere joke for me, to be sure there was no "child lost," but there was this: I made good use of it in keeping the inside track on some things, among which was the right to distribute dodgers, notices, etc., and when Mr. Block and Mr. Cone moved in for a week's campaign, selling ready made clothing and gent's furnishing goods or anything like that, I was the boy to walk through all the streets in town ringing the old Lansing house bell and crying: "Auction! auction! auction! tonight, three doors south of the Lansing house; auction!" and in this way gathered in many Spanish quarters which, with any other gains, were added to the family sinking fund (father did the sinking) for father was a "business man." He kept John Oatly's father busy much of the time painting little signs advertising the many kinds of bake stuffs, bottled beer (soft), etc., on sale at the little red bakery on East Washtenaw street.

You must bear in mind that this was over 50 years ago, long before the city's remarkable growth. It was about this time that Nehemiah came here. I think Nehemiah must certainly have visited Lansing for he says: "Now the city was large and great, but the people were few therein and the houses were not builded."

Leg Is Broken; Cut It Off.

The first surgical operation to be performed in Lansing took place at the house of Dr. Goucher, which stood where the Downey hotel dining room is now, on West Washtenaw street, and the victim was one Elisha Briggs, a stranger in town, whose leg was broken accidentally in alighting from the stage. He was taken into Dr. Goucher's office for care and treatment. The doctor said he had never set a broken leg, nor arm as for that matter, but he thought he could cut it off, and, according to his opinion that would be the best thing to do, anyway. Accordingly he secured the assistance of Dr. Crawford and the twain cut the unfortunate man's leg off the best they could. Of course, the man died. The stranger had a well-filled purse on his person and the doctors took charge of the purse and a young man by the name of Daniel W. Buck took charge of the remains and buried them in the Potters' field in the village cemetery, Cedar street and Michigan avenue, now East Side park. The Potters' field was down near a frog pond, now the artificial lake. It was only a few blocks south of this that one Oliver Rice was terribly frightened a few years later. O. A. Jenison was grading down a sand hill preparatory to building himself a home. Oliver was working on the job and with his team was scraping. He ran his scraper plump under the skeleton of an Indian that had been buried there, the skeleton heading straight for Oliver's face. Having the lines around his neck he could not extricate himself in time to avoid a collision with the aborigine, and he fell face foremost on top of what there was of this noble redman. To say there were no bones broken would be a mistake. There were, but the breakage was wholly sustained by the savage, whose long black hair decorated Mr. Rice's face for about a minute. There was a large turtle shell on the breast of the skeleton with 22 notches cut in the outer edges of the shell. Whether these notches indicated the age of the Indian or were only a tally of the number of scalps he had taken, must forever remain a conjecture. Dr. H. B. Shank secured the skeleton.

Of course, many of the old residents will easily call to mind the many angling roads in and about town. There was the Canada settlement road, converging from Franklin avenue near Washington avenue and running southwesterly, crossing the "forty acres," then west on the state road (Saginaw street) a few miles, then bearing southwesterly to the township of Oneida. This was the route taken by a small colony of Canadians from the Dominion to the promised land, Oneida. Another road running without regard to streets, or lot lines, left the state road near Bogus swamp, angling southeast and intersecting with Michigan avenue near the site of the postoffice. The Battle Creek road was, and is yet, an angling road for a few miles out, as is also the old Detroit and Lansing road, which was planked with good two-inch oak plank by the "Detroit and Lansing Plank Road

Co.," of which James Turner was the president and principal stockholder. This was a toll road and toll gates were established at certain points. There was still another angler, from the east end of Main street, wending its way through the woods northeasterly and crossing the Cedar river where the east city limits touch it, then running north to the Detroit and Lansing road. For the most part these roads followed old Indian trails.

Making a "Pung."

Among the many home-made conveniences of the early settlers was what was known as a "pung" for a winter runabout. The pung was built in this way: Take two long, straight green poles long enough for runners and thills, peel the bark from the poles, cut a slight calf at the point where they are to become thills so that they will bend easily to the proper elevation, bore good-sized auger holes in the top side of the runners, take three good strong pieces for cross beams, bore holes through the ends, use six stanchions or knees, tenant each end, drive three of these into each runner and slip on your cross beams, having the tenants at top end of knees long enough to receive the "rails" which are long enough to reach the thills and fasten to a cross bar, all connections to fit tight; drive together and wedge your tenants and you have your "pung," without an ounce of iron, even a nail, and without a penny's expense. Now go to the store and procure a large dry goods box, fasten this onto your frame and you are ready to hook on.

And, now, I guess I will tell you my experience with one of these improvised vehicles. I happened to be able to locate one of these things, also to locate a horse. Christmas was only twelve hours away. Tom and Joe Hobs, two genial, fun-loving blacksmiths, had the horse. I interviewed these two friends and secured the loan of the horse readily. Now, this horse—well, I think it was one of the worst looking animals I ever saw—large and bony. In fact, the bones and hide were about all there was of it except his head, which was extraordinarily large, and his tail was nearly bald. I secured two good boys, Tom McNeal and Sile Livingston, to join me in the enterprise and next morning, which was Chritsmas, 1849, we went up to Mr. Frary's, captured the "pung" and hauled it down to the shop. The Hobses backed old "Barney" out of his stable under the shop and fitted him up with what scant harness there was. During this preparatory making ready Joe Hobs remarked that "Barney" had (the only thing to recommend him) a most beautiful mane, but it was so matted and bunched up with burrs from running at large during the summer that it resembled a rat. Tom took the bed-cord lines and drove poor old "Barney" up onto the street and we were soon hooked on and loaded in, after attaching to "Barney's" neck the bell that I slyly slipped off our spotted cow on leaving home. Well, the road to glory lay due south and down River street to Main. Turning west we halted and took aboard two Tom-boy girls about our age and bubbling over with fun—then on to Washington avenue, thence north the length of the street to Franklin.

Triumphal Entry.

Out of our respect for old age we had given "Barney" his own gait so far, but as we neared the corner of Franklin avenue, Sile, who wielded the gad, laid it onto poor old "Barney" in order to make as good an appearance as possible on entering the village. But, alas, by some unaccountable mistake on Tom's part, he lost control of the steering apparatus and over we went into the snow, all in a big heap. There was enough of us to make one big heap, but not enough for two. However, no harm done. "Barney" stopped promptly at the word whoa; was very good about that. In fact, he would often stop without it. Well, we were having lots of fun and to make a long story short, we finally doubled the route, drove back with the girls, pulling up at the Michigan house, where the landlord and others were out witnessing our fun. John Thomas, proprietor, ordered "Stuttering Bob" to "take that half-starved beast into the stable and fill him up" (all this with appropriate expletives peculiar only to John Thomas) and took the bunch of us in to a Christmas dinner, where we partook of roast turkey, killed by Mr. Thomas the day previous at a "turkey shoot." So ended our novel Christmas celebration. Yes, we had some fun as long ago as that.

I am reminded at this instance of one stanza of an old-time song I have often heard my mother sing. It was this:

Why should we at our lot complain
  And render life a curse?
Let us take it as you would a wife,
  For better or for worse.
Let us cheerful be, as formilee,
  Be innocently gay
And since we are here with friends so dear
  Let us drive dull care away.

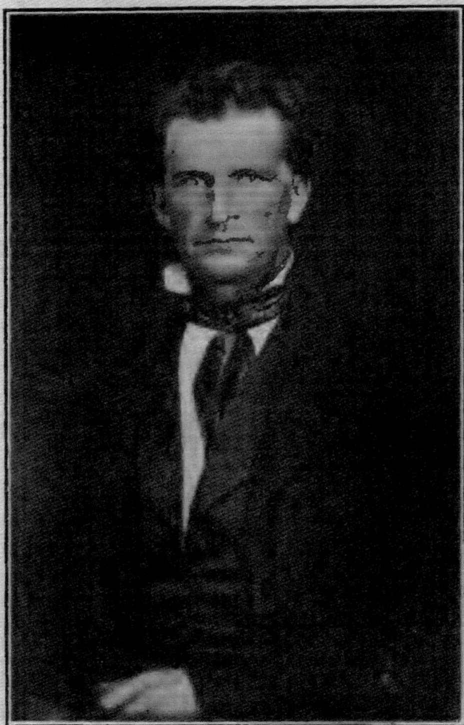

J. C. BAILEY
Pioneer Banker
1848

CUT OFF THUMB INSTEAD.

Tender Hearted Man Turned His Head as Axe Fell On Chicken's Neck.

Life to many is like a pleasant dream, while to some it is for the most part a veritable nightmare. But to a great majority of mankind it seems to run on an intermediate course, partaking alternately of each of these extremes, possibly from the fact that life is largely what we make it. Notwithstanding this is very true, yet we are all liable to accidents and incidents beyond our control that often interrupt the peaceful flow of the best regulated life. I would like to mention one of these accidental incidents in the life of a worthy pioneer, before the dawn of the earliest 50's. On Washington avenue and Shiawassee street in a log cabin lived a very pious and gentle-mannered little man by the name of Wheaton. There came a time when this gentleman's wife was sick, and my mother, who was an old-time nurse, was sent for.

Now, there was a quaint little man living in what was known as Tetertown, a locality on South Sycamore street, taking its name from the first settler in that locality, Anson Teter. This gentleman, who was well known to every one in town as David McAlpin, was celebrated for many good qualities, among which was his cherry disposition and his readiness to help others. He was very handy at butchering parties, and anything in that line. Well, Mrs. Wheaton got along all right and, when sufficiently convalescent, ordered chicken broth. Mr.

Wheaton was called upon to slay a chicken. Now, this was asking a great deal of Mr. Wheaton. He had never taken the life of any living thing and could not have the courage to do so now, notwithstanding the exigency of the case. Accordingly, he summoned his boy Willie and sent him up through the woods to invite Mr. McAlpin to come down and kill the chicken. Mr. McAlpin was disgusted, to say the least, and sent back word to the faint-hearted man to that effect, and there seemed to be no dodging the issue, and he must commit the crime himself. So, with Willie's help he captured his victim and taking the doomed bird to a big stump and holding his neck in proper position with one hand and the up-raised ax with the other, he turned his head for the moment that he might not see the deadly act and then let the ax come down. As might be expected, he missed the chicken and cut his thumb nearly half off and "Biddy" escaped decapitation.

Fell Tree to Get Coons.

It is possible that some of the older residents may remember an immense oak log lying along the roadside just west of the city on Saginaw street, adjacent to the Huxtable farm, having lain there for many years as a monument to the enterprise of the Phillips family. This family consisted in part of old Mr. Phillips and his two grown-up sons, who settled in that vicinity in the early 40's, clearing a few acres and building a cabin. These men were notoriously lazy, eking out a livelihood by raising a little corn, a few turnips, or anything that required but little hard work, killing game, and "cooning," generally by night. Now, the history of that oak tree: One dark, stormy night the dogs began to bark and the boys thought they could hear the peculiar whistle of coon. Hastily dressing, they seized the old tin lantern with its tallow dip, and with ax and gun sallied forth into the darkness, being guided by the barking of the dogs which led them to this historic tree. Satisfied that there was a coon in that monster oak they fell at it with a seeming relish, and worked as though they were working on contract until broad daylight, when the cracking of the tree and the eagerness of the dogs gave unmistakable evidence of success, and they were rewarded for their hard night's work with three coon. Now the consistency—two men working all night to fell a tree measuring four feet across the stump, for three coon (worth 25 cents per coon), men too lazy to cut firewood enough at the door to keep the pot boiling, or to bring it in when cut.

MARIA—Now dear reader, this is not that nocturnal call from the woodshed roof, or from under the back porch, don't think it. No, this is the name of a dear old pioneer friend of the long ago, though I would not infer for a moment that the lady is old by any means. However, when I meet one of these ancient acquaintances it calls back into vivid recollection many for a time forgotten incidents, that carry the mind back as in a flash over many long years, and a paltry half century amounts to hardly a hyphen on the page of life. But to do justice to my erstwhile girl friend of the eighteenth century, let me say that there are few girls that go on dress parade that can or do make as sprightly an appearance and fine figure as Mrs. Marie Sanford or Mrs. Sarah Merrífield and a few other ante-bellum dames, who are so well known among us that their names, so woven into the city's history, have long since become household words.

I had promised to make mention of a few of the more notable of the old-timers who have gone, long since, across the divide, and whom unless we are very good we may never see again, and some, perhaps, we may never wish to, especially our creditors. However, I shall expect, when I join the Lansing colony over there to meet again a great many of the old pioneers that I had known and associated with here.

Feared Wind Storms.

You will undoubtedly remember E. E. Beebe, one of our then most eccentric business men, who built him a home over on Cedar street, mostly under ground, on account of his extreme fear of wind storms, and who was wont to express his views on political and social questions in such a peculiar and striking manner that it raised in your mind grave doubts as to his sanity, and yet he was one of the best men in town. And then there was kind-hearted old Dr. D. G. McClore, who built and ran a drug store on the site of the Hollister block. How I pitied the poor old man one morning soon after the building was finished: some vandal had painted, in large letters on the cornice, "Hay, oats and stabling," while the old doctor slept. Of course, it was a painfully plain building, and did resemble a stable, but it grieved the old gentleman very much and he offered twenty-five cents reward for the perpetrator. The store finally burned down. During the burning the old man was so bent on saving his wines and liquors that he forgot a certain tin box under his bed in the back room containing money and valuable papers, all of which went up in smoke, together with a wad of bank notes, hid in the cellar wall. However, all the high wines were saved, as was also the old box stove on the first floor, his mortar and his pestle. I can easily remember the last time I was in the store; it was rather early in the morning. I was after a half pound of sulphur (mother had the molasses); we were doctoring for the Michigan itch. The old man was splitting matches and cursing the rats. They had very nearly destroyed a small roll of bills the doctor had hid away in some crack or corner for safe keeping. This seemed to be his peculiar banking system.

I remember the first tramp that we ever had any experience with. It was about the first of June, 1848, when a tall, gaunt looking man of possibly 50 years, called upon us and asked for something to eat and lodging for the night. Mother told him that we had been to supper and had but a poor show for a very stylish meal, but had plenty of plain food. Such as it was, he was welcome to it. She set on what there was left, enough for any two ordinary men. He drew up to the table, remarking, "Madame, it isn't quality, it's quantity I'm after," and by the time he had satisfied himself we were convinced that he was right, for he cleaned up on everything before him. His story was that he had left Ionia that morning, where he had been to enter some land. Heading for Lansing he became lost in the woods and only found his way out when reaching this settlement. The government land office was then located at Ionia, and the land this man located has been known more recently as the Peninsular farm, just south of the Agricultural college, owned and cleared of its timber by H. Jipson, who built and operated for many years the "Lansing House," the first hotel where for many years Jate Miller was clerk, Otis Fall was steward and general roustabout. Charles Gilbert was stage agent, office first door south, and H. J. Donahue, second door south, conducted a one-table billiard room and a two-table restaurant and poker parlor. And next, going south, was A. W. Williams' jewelry establishment and then Edgar's bowling alley, and a little farther on was Stanley Briggs' general store. The first livery and sales stable was located on East Washtenaw street, about 113, F. Larue, proprietor.

I feel safe to say that I have been intimately acquainted with several scores of the earliest settlers here during my lifetime, and I love to go down into my memory frequently and stir them up as it were, to set them up in rows, to look them over, and call them by name, and call to mind their virtues and the many good things they had done in their lifetimes, and above all their stalwart heroism in braving the hardships of an almost unbroken wilderness to hew out homes for themselves and lay the foundations for the luxurious homes for their posterity and for the "stranger within our gates." I am proud that it has been my happy fortune to witness the rise and development of Michigan's capital city. I am proud of its founders, I am proud of their commendable records of endurance, their patience and ultimate success.

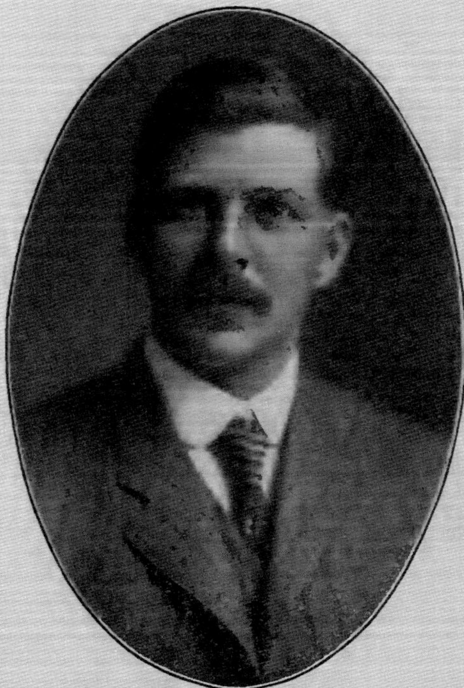

R. E. OLDS
Pioneer inventor, gasoline engines, Pres. Reo Motor Car Company

LIVES OF EARLY SETTLERS.

Biographical Sketches of Some of Early Residents of Years Ago.

Possibly the most unique, if not one of the most eccentric celebrities among the earliest of the old settlers was Col. Joseph Moon, known by his relatives as "Uncle Joe." Being distantly related to my family, I feel the more free to speak of him, actuated possibly by a modest pride that he was a second cousin to my mother and understood the manual of arms as well as any old veteran and often entertained the boys gathered around him (when he was feeling valiant) with an exhibition of his military skill and thrilling tales of his exploits and escapes in "the times that tried men's souls," marching, it might be, shoulder to shoulder with "George," as he familiarly referred to General Washington. Oh, how it made our young hearts swell with patriotic valor and made us feel proud of our American soldiery, proud of our historic ancestors, proud of the colonel. Uncle Joe was a great warrior, but this was not the extent of his greatness, for he loved peace also, and plied himself industriously at coopering in his shop adjacent to his cabin. He was also a doctor of the botanical school, having great faith in herbs and roots, believing as he often averred, "they can do no hurt if they do no good."

My father sent me up to the colonel's one afternoon in early spring to borrow the old gentleman's tapping gouge. I entered through the shop and was passing through the open door into the house when I heard Aunt Jane's emphatic invitation to Uncle Joe to "go long, you old fool," "blow the horn an' get the girls here quick." Now, the "girls" were out in the sap bush, hard at work (they had no boys then) and the colonel was standing in front of the bed with his back toward me as straight as a candle, holding a large wisp of pennyroyal over his "Lady Jane's" nose and saying, "Smell o' that, Lady Jane, the colonel can cure you." Then that nasal injunction would come again and again from "Lady Jane" as the colonel persistently plied his profession, lying down one wisp of herbs and administering another in the same way, heedless of his patient's groans and admonitions. I finally came to the rescue for I saw that Aunt Jane was pretty sick. I blew the horn, ran away and summoned the nearest neighbor, did my errand and left; it was another girl. The colonel was a soldier of the Ethan Allen type; as supple as a circus rider; erect as a lamp post; could walk a line under any circumstance and could kick higher than any other man on the school section; not given to contention yet could produce at times some very convincing arguments. I called there one Saturday evening in February, 1850, and found I was there in time for matinee. The colonel was sitting behind a primitive loom, attired in a cotton shirt and an ancient and buttonless overcoat, while his "Lady Jane" was seated before a red hot stove with a face of the same hue, her eyes gleaming with an unnatural brightness.

I said "Good evening, hello Uncle Joe, taking a foot bath?" The colonel popped up erect and began to explain. "Daniel, my son. The old fool has gone and burnt up his clothes, every dud," broke in Aunt Jane. "You see, Daniel, my son," began Uncle Joe again, "the colonel bought him cloth for a suit of clothes over three years ago and that cloth has laid in the bureau drawer ever since. If the colonel wants to go to church or to see the legislature or anything like that he can't go by—. Nothing but them greasy old worn-out clothes that I've worn ever since we came to Michigan. I guess she'll get at it now and make um up." I thought the colonel's argument was conclusive.

He owned a lot on Sycamore street. One day when he was feeling extremely warlike, he hied him down town and exchanged this lot with a certain gunsmith for a job lot of guns of different kinds and calibers, purposing to build a stockade around his cabin and with this arsenal to be ready to repel any attack from the Indians or the British, who he imagined would some day fall upon Detroit. Taking that they would naturally sweep westward, intent on taking the capitol, he proposed to be ready for any emergency. He would drill his girls in the art of war and the manual of arms to such efficiency that they would be able to shoot as far and as straight as any "Britisher."

I have been asked for a life-like description of old Chief Okemos as I saw him. He was short, stout built and slow in his movements, very stern and the beau-ideal of the typical savage. His face was deeply furrowed by extreme age, with many battle scars, the one most prominent was the lobe of one ear which hung dangling from the main organ. He had eyes which still retained their wartime fierceness. He dressed in buckskin leggins and moccasins, with a well-worn sash tied about his waist, from which a weasel skin tobacco pouch and a long scalping knife were suspended. This, with a dirty turban about his head, constituted his wardrobe.

I well remember the first time I saw him—it was in the spring of '48. Father was shaping up a store trough from a fine basswood log on Saginaw street. The old warrior with two stalwart bucks drew near and halted, watching father as if curious to know what he intended to do with the log. Father, of course, ceased his work and undertook to converse with them, speaking mainly in an unknown tongue of broken German mixed with hog-latin. This seemed to astonish the natives. Finally father asked Mr. Okemos in plain English, "How old a man are you?" The old chief said never a word, but squared away and with his arms outstretched counted off one hundred in Indian mathematics. Every movement was a moon and every cycle of moons was a year. This pleased father so much that he stepped a little to one side and running his hand down into a hollow stump drew up a quart bottle and passed it over to the old gent in consideration, likely of his having, notwithstanding all his hardships, attained this ripe old age. Chief Okemos seized the proffered "hospitality" with an eagerness known only to the red man and pulling the cork put it to his nose, put it to his mouth, gave the conventional grunt, and then the three Indians about faced and disappeared into the depths of the forest, taking the bottle with them. The old chief seldom came to town with the rest of the tribe, being somewhat feeble, especially after they moved down to Chimna-Con, where they built them log cabins similar to those of the whites, where they lived, or rather died. There are very few, if any, left of that remnant of a once powerful and savage tribe, which was an ally of the great Chieftain Pontiac, own uncle of the blood-thirsty subject of this short sketch, Okemos.

Major Williams was another war-like character and had his eccentricities. He gloried in having been a volunteer in the patriot war. Banished by the British government he was released and returned to America by the strenuous efforts of his son, A. W. Williams, Lansing's first jeweler. The major delighted in training with the boys on the Fourth of July and usually fired the anvil for us, but had it in for me from the first, for dropping a handful of lighted firecrackers into his coat pocket while on the firing line. He chased me into the woods and out again, and more too, with the hot touching-off iron, swearing he would burn a hole in my hide if he caught me, and I never felt safe in his presence until I attended his funeral. He was eccentric all right enough. The old gentleman built a great boat, a real propeller, the first power boat that ever graced the fair bosom of the Grand in the corporate limits of this city. It was a side-wheeler and the wheels were driven by pump handles attached to cranks, exclusively a man-power craft. Two strong men at the pump handles could by working very hard propel the boat for quite a distance if they had the time. It afforded the young people great sport to take Sunday excursions on the "Experiment," as the major was pleased to name it. Major Williams was an expert in "hiving bees," and discovered many a bee tree well stored with honey. Once upon a time while "hiving" he came suddenly upon a large swarm gathered in a great bunch on a stub, just in the edge of a clearing west of town. The major was delighted, went hastily to the nearest cabin, engaged a lad to help him, borrowed a box, a barrel and a tablecloth and returned to the stub intent upon hiving those bees. It occurred to him that he had heard that to blow tobacco smoke among them that it would so deaden the bees that they could be easily taken.

"Does your father smoke?" he asked the boy.

"Yes, sir."

"Run back and get a pipe, well filled, and some matches. Hurry, my boy."

The lad was soon back. The major lighted the pipe and mounted the barrel, and he smoked and he smoked, blew and blew again and again among the honey makers, but without any apparent effect on them. It was different with the major, he soon became deathly sick and dismounting lay down on the ground. The boy was frightened, ran for the cabin and told his father, who had just come in from his chopping for his dinner, and the kindly woodman immediately yoked up his cattle and hooking onto a sled, drove over and drew the poor major home, a very sick man and very badly stung. This was the first and the last smoke for Major Williams. I attended the major's funeral a few years later, following him to his last resting place. The cemetery was then at Michigan avenue and Cedar street, the township board having located it over there in order to have it "forever remote" from the resident part of the town.

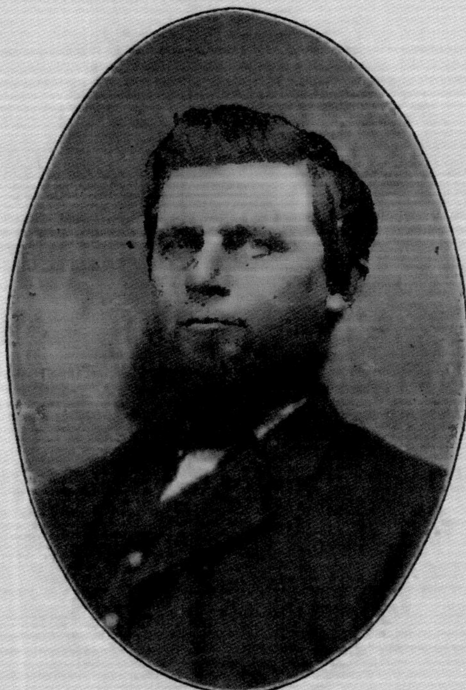

ISRAEL GILLET
Pioneer Jeweler and Architect

OLD-FASHIONED TOILETS.

Wisp of Sweet Camomile or Rosemary was Formerly Used as a Perfumery.

I attended a social event lately where the dazzling incandescent lights shone over fair women and well attired men, and the volume of the latest and most exquisite perfumery was so dense that it was really nauseating to the innocent minded and more unappreciative ancients present. Of course young people can and will tolerate more of this kind of excess of a great social evil than their elders, who have not been educated up to the high standard of the modern dude. As I said, I attended, but becoming surfeited with the odors I was obliged to beg to be excused. Returning home I lost no time in climbing to my room in the attic and found a welcome repose in the old wooden rocker, an heirloom in my grandfather's family, the one in which my mother rocked all of her ten babies to sleep in. I was soon in a retrospective mood, very naturally, and my mind went back to more primitive times and more simple and more sensible toilets. In the olden time ladies were wont to pack their wardrobe in a chest or drawer, and repairing to the garden would gather a goodly wisp of sweet camomile or some rosemary, a quince, in short any or all of these or other aromatics, and packed among the clothing would permeate the whole wardrobe with a very delicate and pleasing aroma, and not infrequently the lady would slip something of this sort into her dress pocket in the event of attending a ball or other function and anon flirt her kerchief, drawn from this pocket, in the face of her escort, to add, no doubt, to his enjoyment. This, with a liberal application of bear's oil or pomade for the hair, and the toilet was complete.

A Little Incident.

I am reminded of a little incident of the very early fifties. The bar room office of the Lansing house was a gathering place for many of the old-time worthies, especially in the long winter evenings. On one occasion there was the usual circle around the great box stove, exchanging gossip, telling of the hunt or other stories, when in came Nelse Edgar, the town's only dude. A new and expensive perfume, known as "musk," had struck the elite of our little burg, and Nelt had discovered it, and of course used it, used it generously. It was a new thing to the squad of old fogies around the stove, among whom was the war-like Col. Joseph Moon of Teter-town. The intense heat of the red hot stove compelled the crowd to move back, and as Nelt warmed up, so did the "perfume." Soon the colonel was moved with compassion for Mr. Edgar, and drawing up close to his side in a very confidential way, began to commiserate him on his misfortune.

He says: "Nelson, my son, the colonel was once in just such a fix himself. About a year ago last fall, along in the night, my lady Jane awoke the colonel and she says: 'Joseph, there is something wrong going on out in that air hen roost.' I got right up, pulled on my pants and lit the lantern, and then I took down my rifle and out to the chicken coop I went, and sure enough there he was as true as guns. Well, I sat down the lantern, and up with the rifle and let go at him, at the same time jumping on him with both feet. I hadn't otto hev done that, for he wasn't dead yet. I wished he was, for I got so bespattered, well I smelt worse than you do now. A neighbor told me to bury my clothes for three days and three nights. So I went to bed and my lady Jane buried my clothes for me, and in three days I got up and put them on. They were all right again."

However, "Nelse" did not get this last chapter of the colonel's advice. He was out and walking up the street very fast. Albeit I am aware that in this age of the world's rapid gait, socially it becomes almost a necessity that one should be "perfumed" to a certain extent to be "strictly modern," but like many other fashionable fads, it may be largely overdone, and to that extent that it ceases to be a pleasure and becomes a nuisance which should be by rights referred to the board of health for abatement. However, as for the "camomile bed," rosemary, etc., of which all well regulated homes of the olden time were supplied, these with many other ancient, harmless commodities and useful medicinal herbs have long since been relegated to the apothecary's shop and it has become more convenient to call on these for a little of the "tincture" or extract.

A Little Confession.

It has often been said, and perhaps truly, that "confession is good for the soul." I know it is for the conscience. Like a liberal dose of malt whiskey, it often gives instant relief, and I will, with your permission, make a clean breast of an unintentional nearness to committing the crime of manslaughter, or more properly speaking, boy-slaughter, and blowing the soul, and body too, as for that matter, of one of the best boys the city ever boasted, not excepting myself. This is the story. A certain merchant in this city employed this young lad as clerk, partly on account of his innate honesty and amiable disposition, for in the words of Timothy Coffee, in eulogizing Mr. E. M. Thorpe, that "he is a gintleman, himself and his wife." Our boy had no wife, however. He had all the gentlemanly attributes aside from this. One of the conditions of servitude bound the boy to sleep in the store, and do you know what it means to sleep in a large grocery store? Simply suicidal to say nothing of its more or less (and generally more) sickening atmosphere. The boy was faithful to his trust, without a whimper for a long time, until a most fortunate circumstance which changed the current of his whole life. Your uncle was employed for some time in the same establishment as "help." One Saturday afternoon, Gilkey, the cartage man, came with a load of goods, among which were several kegs of powder. It was a very busy day and too late to take the powder away to its place outside the city and Dan was ordered to hustle the stuff down below in a hurry, for to keep all that amount of explosive matter in the store over night would be an infringement on the insurance policy. I was instructed to stack it up on the big bench. Now on this bench were several boxes of lemons. In the evening on my first trip down for lemons I lighted a candle as usual, set the candle on the corner of a box partly full of lemons and about seven or eight inches from this stack of powder. I was down after lemons several times, fully expecting to bring up the light on the last trip, but of course forgot to do so. The lad's couch was directly over this bank of powder, lemons and candle. Imagine my consternation on the following Monday to discover that the candle had burned down into the socket, the molten grease burning on its flow down into the box and the box itself burned down to its very bottom, and I must believe that nothing short of the interposition of divine providence saved a terrible and fatal catastrophe and saved to Lansing one of her most honorable benefactors, one of her most charitable and humanitarian citizens, whose crowning glory is erecting for the city and for suffering humanity a magnificent hospital, which will stand a grand monument to his munificent, great-hearted generosity. All honor to the city's greatest benefactors, the names of E. W. Sparrow and J. H. Moores and a few more yet to be heard from, will go down to posterity as household words, and a grateful remembrance through the remaining annals of the city's history.

"Little drops of water,
  Little grains of sand,
Make the mighty ocean
  And the great big land."

Acts of Kindness Tell in End.

Just so, and little acts of kindness, mercy and charity are a good index to a man's inner nature. I recall one incident in the everyday life of this man, Sparrow, which is very characteristic of the man, as I have known him through an acquaintance of 40 years or more. It was related to me confidentially. Mr. Sparrow owned a tract of timbered land adjoining the city. There lived near this land a very poor and very industrious man with a sick wife and a number of children. It was a severely cold winter, and this poor man was out of employment. His resources were exhausted, and being a comparative stranger, was too modest to ask for credit for fear of denial. There were several ranks of wood in the timber nearby. His family was suffering with the cold. He helped himself to a small portion of one of these wood piles in his distress, promising himself that when he should get to work again he would seek out the owner and pay him for the wood. Mr. Sparrow's agent discovered the seeming theft, in fact saw the man in the very act, and very promptly reported the matter, expecting that Mr. Sparrow would cause his arrest immediately. Not so. Mr. Sparrow asked his faithful game keeper how much wood there was left. He replied that there was about one and a half cords.

"Load the balance of that wood onto your wagon in the morning and draw it over to his house and throw it off, and say nothing about it to anyone," said Mr. Sparrow.

As soon as the poor man found employment, the first thing he did was to repair to the proprietor's office and offer to pay for the wood, leaving the office much happier than he came. How much better thus than to have appealed to the courts and cause that poor man to be imprisoned, ruining the unfortunate derelict and sinking his family into an everlasting disgrace. This same man has proved to be an upright, exemplary citizen. Oh, for a greater display of this kindly forbearance of man toward his brother man.

A Tale About a Pup.

Let me tell you a little story. One fine morning, back in forty-nine, I think it was, Billy Lobdell, a boy chum, and I were wandering through the woods up on Capitol avenue. We came upon a stray puppy and in the kindness of our hearts we picked him up, fearing some irreverent boy might steal the little thing. We walked on for about a block or two and sat down upon a log. We would both like to own the pup. Billy made the proposition that the one that could tell the biggest lie should take the beast. While we were working at this, along came old Elder Merril. He stopped to admire our prize, and Billy, the dunce, up and told him what we were about, and well, you should have seen that elder. He stood himself up full length and throwing up both hands in holy horror, he began to preach to us. He gave us the Washington story. I interrupted him here by making the remark that George was probably the only boy at that early period of our country's history that could not tell some kind of a lie if he tried right hard. However, the elder kept on talking and wound up with saying: "Boys, look at me, a man over 60, and I never told a lie in my life."

I says, "Billy, give the elder the pup."

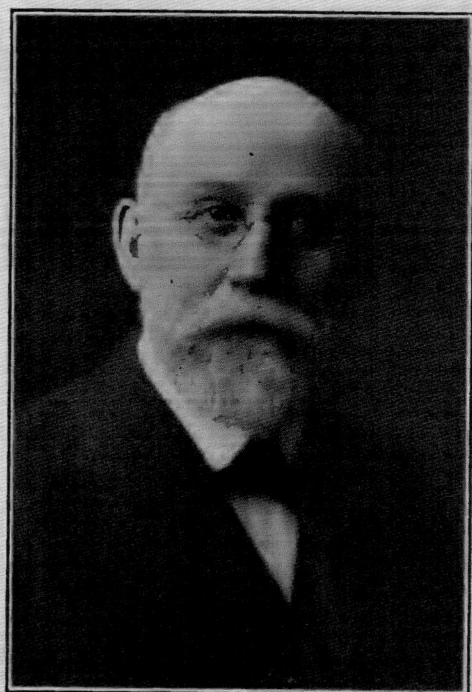

J. H. MOORES
Capitalist and Real Estate

HISTORICAL SKETCH OF CITY.

Directory of Some of the Old Timers Who Lived in Lansing Prior to 1855.

I have been requested by a number of the readers of The State Journal to give them a little historical sketch of the city in the first few years from its foundation. I will endeavor to do this as best I can, if you will keep in mind the fact that though ordinarily truthful, comparatively speaking, and not unlike the majority of the human family, liable to mistakes, I too might utter an unintentional error. However, I will undertake to tell you only what I know to be true. And now, if every one would do that, what a better understanding we would all have of existing conditions and past experiences. Mountains would shrink again to molehills, and fish stories would cease to interest.

If the "casual observer" would pause and consider the "lay of the land," he would discover no doubt that the original city as laid out by our forefathers was situated on an island, bounded on the north by Jones' lake and a cranberry marsh; on the east by the Cedar river and the artificial lake in the East Side park; on the south by the hogsback and the Dimondale dam; and on the west by the Bogus swamp. It was settled by Americans and down-easters, with here and there a red man. Having driven the savages out with a shotgun, these natives were a docile race and possessed a considerable native modesty and timidity. I have often seen them dodge down behind a stump or tree to shoot, with not a man, black or white, within a hundred rods.

Advice to Mr. Seymour.

In the years when Horatio Seymour was Tetrarch of York state, his brother, James, being out of a job, sought Horatio's advice and assistance, both of which he obtained. Horatio says to Jim: "Go west. Go to Michigan. There is a new state, flowing with the finest of opportunities, well timbered and traversed by great rivers and nearly surrounded by the great lakes. It has every facility for accumulating a fortune. Go into the interior of this new state, and locate a tract of land on some good river, with water power. Build a dam. Build a saw mill. Lay out your land into town lots, advertise and make a hustle. In fact, build a town and make yourself independent."

James took Horatio's advice, and found his Eldorado on the section adjoining section 16 on the north, bought it and proceeded to build a dam, a saw mill, etc., and create a town. The same is known as North Lansing. Two years later the people of the state of Michigan concluded to start a new capitol, and decided to put it down beside Mr. Seymour's town, not as a competitor of the new town, but on account of the conveniences already on the ground, a dam, a saw mill, a log grocery, and steps taken for the establishment of a cemetery. All the inducements necessary for the founding of a city, all of which satisfied the commissioners, who were appointed by the governor to locate the new capitol, that this was the proper locality, geographically and strategically to launch the new enterprise.

Hence, the stakes were set at once, and the stump machine was put in operation. A clearing was made, and a building erected. Town lots were staked out and another town spread upon the map. Meantime a company was organized, known as the Bush, Thomas & Lee combination, who obtained title to the section on the south of the state's plat. This company proceeded forthwith to create another town, in competition with these two already under way. This was known for many years as "upper town," finally all three towns, working on the grand principle of reciprocity having so prospered and pushed out their borders until now they have consolidated and we are known only as the city of Lansing, one of the most beautiful cities in the state, and still growing and spreading like the proverbial bay tree. And this is the whole thing in a nutshell.

Some Old Timers.

It may be of interest to some to mention the names of some of the earliest settlers of Lansing prior to 1855. The following is a partial list of those that I call to mind at this time. There is a possibility of some mistakes, but I think it is pretty nearly correct, as far as it goes. They are these:

Atterburry, Rev.
Alton, Frederick
Alton, Augustus
Armstrong, C. S.
Armstrong, George
Armes, Ormel
Armes, Henry
Allen, Charles F.
Bush, John N.
Bush, Charles P.
Bush, Isaac
Bingham, S. D.
Brown, Abner
Brown, N. A.
Butler, Orange
Butler, Charles W.

Barker, Wilfred
Bradford, John
Billings, T. D.
Baker, Harvey
Bush, John J.
Bell, Digby V.
Burdick, I. H.
Buck, Daniel W.
Bartholomew, I. H.
Bartholomew, Henry
Bailey, J. C.
Briggs, Stanley
Briggs, James
Briggs, Richard
Bennett, Cy
Bennett, John N.
Bagley, A. B.
Beal, George
Bagley, D. M.
Burner, Gotloeb
Bascom, James
Bascom, Rollin
Briggs, Warren
Burt, Oliver
Baker, J. H.
Beebe, E. E.
Cooley, Fred
Coryell, Samuel S.
Coryell, Cyrus
Cowles, J. P.
Cowels, F. M.
Cowles, Albert E.
Cutler, A. D.
Christopher, John
Christopher, George
Childs, John
Childs, Mark
Cooley, Lansing
Carr, John A.
Carr, William M.
Clapsadle, R. W.
Carpenter, M. B.
Carpenter, H. B.
Carpenter, H. C.
Calkins, Andrew
Christmas, John
Chapman, William M.
Darling, Christopher C.
Darling, John
Dart, R. C.
Dart, Ebbin
Dearin, A. V.
Dearin, Simeon
Dodge, C. C.
Dingman, John
Dunks, H. H.
Edgar, Dennis
Edgar, Nelson
Ellis, Thomas
Ellis, William
Eckstine, David
Ewer, Firby
Elliott, Richard
Eliot, Edward.
Fall, Otis C.
Faxon, Wm. C.
Foster, Geo. J.
Foster, Theodore
Foster, Seymour
Foster, Wm.

Foote, Geo. E.
Ferley, Henry
Gibson, Rodney
Godly, John
Godly, Elder
Greene, T. W.
Grass, Jacob
Gibbs, Henry
Gilkey, O. H.
Grilley, Ed.
Grove, Geo. K.
Greene, S. R.
Gilkey, Wm.
Gordon, Harvey
Havens, Champion
Hawley, Dr.
Harmon, John O.
Holmes, Jas. W.
Hilliard, James
Haze, Wm. H.
Hart, A. N.
Hart, Benjamin
Hulse, Albert
Hinman, Wm.
Hedges, Chas. C.
Ingersol, Harley
Irish, Welcome
Jipson, Henry
Jennings, R. D.
Johnson, Wm.
Johnson, Dr.
Jackson, Andrew
Jenison, O. A.
Jennison, L. S.
Jones, Ezra
Jones, Whitney
Jordan, Richard
Johnson, Daniel
Kerr, John A.
Kilbourne, S. L.
Longyear, John W.
Longyear, Ephriam
Longyear, Stephen D.
Little, Wm.
Ledrer, Manuel
Lobdel, J. H.
Long, John
Longbon, David
Lovejoy, Capt.
Ledrer, Henry
Murry, Geo. R.
McAlpin, David
Miller, Jason E.
McGivern, Wm.
Morehouse, Thomas
Morehouse, A. H. P.
Mead, Jas. I.
Merril, T. W.
Miles, James
Myers, J. Walter
McClure, D. G.
Mevis, O. H.
Madden, Squire
Madden, Alpheus
Morehouse, A. H.
Morehouse, Stephen
Miles, J. P.
Moon, Col. Joseph
Murphy, Van S.
Merrifield, E. R.

Newbro, Eugene
Newbro, S. D.
Olds, Wm.
Osband, M. D.
Osband, Edwin
Ostrander
Olds, P. F.
Oatly, John
Osborn, Wm.
Potter, Elder
Peck, Geo. W.
Pritchard, M. N.
Post, J. W.
Pinckney, Wm. H.
Price, John R.
Palmer, Thomas
Potter, Theodore
Page, Jabez
Parker, Daniel
Reece, Robert
Robson, John
Roberts, Isaac
Rankin, J. W.
Robson, Robert
Radick, John I.
Rowley, John I.
Shattuck, Asa
Shattuck, Allen S.
Shattuck, Daniel
Shattuck, Nelson
Sanford, Edward
Smith, Peter
Strouble, Jacob
Smith, Samuel
Smith, Joseph
Starkey, Henry
Sanford, Elijah
Steeples, Geo.
Shubel, Fred
Tooker, Smith
Tooker, Ransom
Tooker, John S.
Terry, Arthur
Thayer, Homer
Teter, Anson
Thomas, John
Turner, James
Turner, Amos
Thayer, A. R.
Veilie, A. J.
Van Buren, Wm.
Warner, J. E.
Wildt, Chas.
Wiswold, Peter
Welch, Tate
Ward, Anson
Ward, Watterman
Ward, U. D.
Williams, A. W.
Wheaton, Wm.
Woodworth, Geo. R.
Wolcot, Alexander C.
Wiser, John
Wescot, David
Westcot, J. W.
Whitely, John
Wakenhoot, Christ
Yeiter, Frederick

Many Others.

There are many more, for as I meditate, their names and phantom faces come trooping over memory's disk, like pleasant specters of a former life, and seem to beckon me again to converse, for with many of them I have enjoyed many a pleasant visit in their life time. I recall just now some of the happiest hours of my young life, spent in the boot and shoe store of that genial and kind hearted cobbler of ye olden time, George R. Woodworth, who will undoubtedly be remembered by some of the old timers, (father of Henry A. Woodworth), how I would sit entranced by the hour and listen to his stories of "York state" lore. His kindly words, so kindly spoken, while he pounded the last or finished off the soles of an "honest pair of boots," or "waited on" some hapless lad who had been sent in by some mischievous neighbor for a little good "strap oil." The kindly old gentleman could never find it in his heart to refuse this. However, he could never accommodate them to a "three cornered last."

Of course there was competition in the boot and shoe business, for certainly no one man could take care of the entire trade, making and mending and tapping for upwards of a thousand persons. Therefore, as early as this we had a shop at the north end, operated by a little German, another up on Main street, with a small sign standing up against the front end of the shop near the little door with a primitive boot and also a shoe represented with this motto over the device: "A. Ward," and under it was this, "Made and Repaired." On East Allegan street was another unpretending shop, owned and operated by a Mr. Morehouse and his son, Stephen, distant relatives of the gentleman from Erin.

These two gentlemen were celebrated for their "lasting" abilities and for being as honest and truthful as was consistent with the business. However, it was well to get your order in and measurements taken at least 30 days prior to the time that you really felt you must have the boots. You were expected to pay one dollar fifty cash, or two dollars in trade for a bang up, good, serviceable pair of boots. There were very few shoes made in those days. A pair of pumps or oxfords occasionally for house wear, and the boot-jack was as indispensible as was the dinner pot. However, the majority of the people could not afford the luxury of boots all the year round, and consequently went bare-footed through the summer months. Of course this meant chapped feet and stone-bruises, etc.

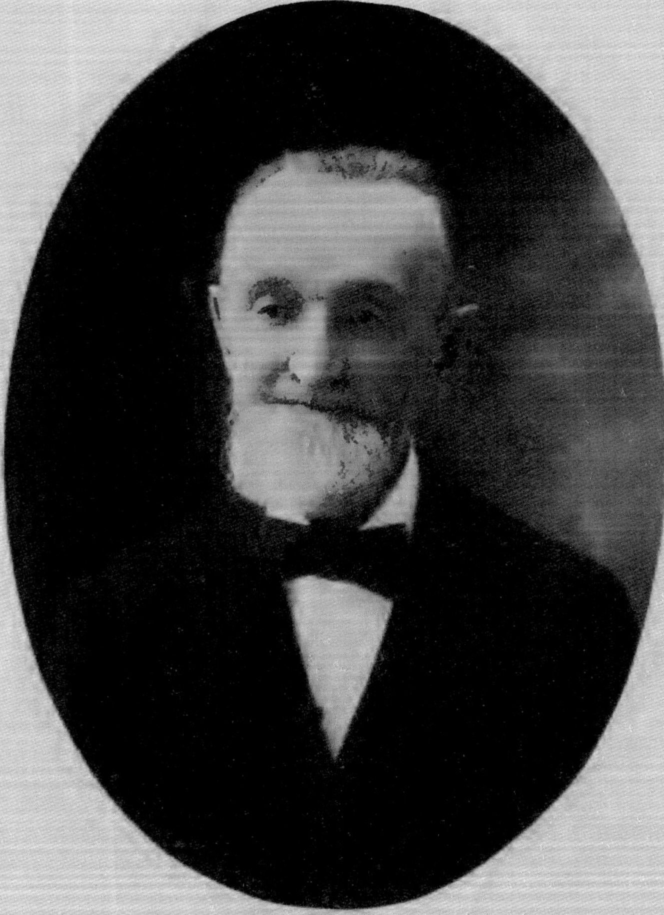

C. B. STEBBINS

Capitalist; for many years Deputy Superintendent of Public Instruction, late Vice President Lansing Wheelbarrow Works

PIONEER BUSINESS MEN.

Proprietors of Mercantile Establishments of Long Ago.

There seems at this late day to be some difference of opinion as to the antiquity of some of the mercantile concerns of the city, more especially as to what grocery could claim the title of the pioneer grocery. While I do not claim to know everything, I do know something. Now, as to the grocery business. According to my recollection it is this: In 1846 some man started the business in a small log cabin on Franklin avenue, near Center street. In 1848, one Levi Hunt built a small, one-story building at about 103 South Washington avenue and brought that log cabin grocery stock up to "middle town" and installed it in this building which was known as Hunt's grocery for many years. On the death of Mr. Hunt, the stock was bought by the Clagget brothers, who conducted the business for a few years when disagreeing to agree they threw up the business and sold to A. B. Bagly, whose failing health compelled him to relinquish the business after a few years when the stock was sold to J. J. Sidway, who conducted the business for a short time, but on account of a little misunderstanding as to the "maine law" and a blind pig or something of that nature, Mr. Sidway went west, the stock being transferred to Messrs. Ferrand and Shank who in the event of the necessity of moving out the old building to give place for the present structure moved across the avenue. In a short time

Mr. R. B. Shank became sole proprietor, and at his death was succeeded by Christopher and Loftus and is now known as the Frank Loftus grocery. I am credibly informed that the original stock of the old Levi Hunt grocery has been superseded by an entire new line of goods, all of which makes this house virtually the pioneer grocery.

Speaking of pioneer business houses brings to my mind several that I can remember very distinctly. If I am not mistaken, the first hardware store that the Capital City could boast of was that of A. N. Hart at the corner of Franklin avenue and Center street. The second was soon after started by Edward Elliot at the corner of Washington avenue and Allegan street. On the demise of Mr. Elliot this store passed into the hands of A. R. Burr and Geo. K. Grove. This store burned down somewhere in the fifties and the firm resumed business in the building vacated by Wright & Holmes, 102 South Washington avenue. On the retirement of Col. A. R. Burr from the business, E. H. Whitney took his interest and the firm name became Grove & Whitney and remained thus until the death of Mr. Grove, in the event of which the affairs of the firm were closed up and the business went into other hands.

In the person of Geo. K. Grove, there is a character among the early pioneers worthy of more than passing notice. Known by nearly every one, young and old, far and near, and who really knew every one in and out of the city within a radius of many miles, virtually a living and live wire, (so to speak), directory, to whom, usually all inquiries were referred concerning any man sought for. He always knew the name, his residence, and in fact as a general thing all about him. Mr. Grove was known to have only one great fault, and this, strictly speaking, was a physical disability; we might diagnose it as an enlargement of the heart. In other words, he was really too generous for his own profit. His hand and his pocket were always open to the distressed and unfortunate, and his sympathy knew no bounds.

Among the people of the early forties there was one man a little more prominent in the development of the infant city than many of the old worthies of the time. In fact, it is undoubtedly true that James Turner, with the assistance of James and Horatio Seymour, was entitled to the credit of inducing the commissioners to locate the new capitol where it now is. Early in 1847 Mr. Turner built the first frame house erected in the now city of Lansing, and strange to say, it is still standing, and on the very site on which it was built, and can be seen on Turner street, first door north of the Lansing Brewing Co., as can also one of three locust trees, raised from the seed and planted by the hand of Mrs. Marion M. Turner, who is still living at the age of 93. Living did I say? Yes, and in possession of all her faculties apparently and all her remarkable grace and womanly beauty, of body and mind, notwithstanding all these long years of pioneer life with its varied experiences, not excepting the successful raising of one of the grandest families a Christian mother was ever blessed with. Surely she has her reward.

Growing Old.

Softly, oh softly the years have swept by thee,
  Touching thee lightly with tenderest care;

Sorrow and death did they often bring nigh thee,
  Yet they have left thee but beauty to wear,
      Growing old gracefully,
      Gracefully fair.

Far from the storms that are lashing the ocean,
  Nearer each day to the pleasant home light
Far from the waves that are big with commotion,
  Under full sail and the harbor in sight,
      Growing old cheerfully,
      Cheerful and bright.

Past all the winds that were adverse and chilling,
  Past all the currents that wooed thee unwilling;
Far from the port and the land of the blest,
      Growing old peacefully,
      Peaceful and blest.

Never a feeling of envy or sorrow
  When the bright faces of children are seen,
Never a year from their youth would'st thou borrow,
  Thou dost remember what lieth between;
      Growing old willingly,
      Gladly I ween.

Rich in experience that angels might covet,
  Rich in a faith that has grown with thy years,
Rich in a love that grew from and above it,
  Soothing thy sorrow and hushing thy fears,
      Growing old wealthily,
      Loving and dear.

Hearts at the sound of thy coming are lightened;
  Ready and willing thy hand to receive;

Many a face at thy kind word has brightened;
"It is more blessed to give than receive;"
Growing old happily,
Blest, we believe.

Eyes that grow dim to the earth and its glory
See but the brighter the heavenly glow;
Ears that are dull to the world and its story
Drink in the songs that from Paradise flow.
All this sweet recompense
Youth cannot know.

Forward, yet softly the years have swept by thee,
Touching thee lightly with tenderest care;
Sorrow and death they did often bring nigh thee,
Yet they have left thee but beauty to wear,
Growing old gracefully,
Graceful and fair.

—Vincent Daws.

Mrs. Turner, whose maiden name was Monroe, is the oldest daughter of a family remarkable for longevity. One sister being 87 at this writing; another sister, Mrs. Webber, being 91, and several other "children" of the Monroe family having long since passed the three score and ten allotment of the human family, all sturdy pioneers of the highest type.

We have with us also the genial Joseph E. Warner, veteran showman and pioneer politician, whose smiling face and cheerful salutation is like a ray of sunshine on a frosty morning, and whose kind words and ready help are a God-send to so many.

One of the most familiar figures and faces for many years was that of the quiet, even tempered

Judge William H. Chapman, who with his ready and ever-present jack-knife, was willing and ready at any and all times to sit down beside you, and after carefully selecting a good, soft pine stick to whittle, and quietly talk over the political situation. Judge Wm. H. Pinckney was of a little different disposition, though no less honorable or well read in matters of law and jurisprudence, and whose decisions were invariably just.

Hon. DeWitt C. Leach was another of Lansing's long-time pioneer citizens, a member of congress, and for some years editor of the Lansing Weekly State Republican. He was succeeded by Mr. Stephen D. Bingham, who was succeeded by J. W. King, who held the chair up to the time that the stalwart journalist W. S. George took charge of the office as managing partner and editor-in-chief. This concern did the state printing by contract for over 50 years.

I have been all things to all men, from first to last, have traveled over some of the world and a part of Canada, and like Capt. Kid I have sailed. Yes, I remember having sailed across Grand river at one time on horse-back, it was in the spring of 1850. The "spring freshet" was upon us as usual, sweeping away the bridges of course. Consequently the settlers could not get to town with their products and there was a dearth of many things, especially that of butter. This circumstance had continued for several weeks, when O. A. Jenison, Rodney Gibson and A. V. Dearin determined to have butter at any cost. Some enterprising men had stretched a great rope across the river at MacKrill point, to which snatch blocks were attached and made fast to a great lumber scow which was operated as a ferry. Mr. Jenison engaged me to go across and search the country for butter, giving me the necessary funds to pay for it and pay my fare on the scow. I was acquainted with good old Mr. North, (the father of all the Norths), and I made a bee line for that sturdy old settler's ranch where I procured the commodity at the moderate price of 40 cents per pound. It proved to be a very fine article, but somewhat expensive. Speaking of Mr. North, reminds me that this old pioneer of the township gave us the name Lansing, having come here from Lansing, N. Y.

There are no days like the good old days,
  The days when we were youthful!
When human kind were pure of mind
  And speech and deeds were truthful;
Before a love for sordid gold
  Became man's ruling passion,
And before each maid and dame became
  Slave to the tyrant Fashion!

There are no girls like the good old girls,
  Against the world I'd stake 'em!
As buxom and smart and clean of heart
  As the Lord knew how to make 'em!
They were rich in spirit and common sense,
  And piety all supportin';
They could bake and brew, and had taught school,
      too
  And they made the likeliest courtin'!

There are no boys like the good old boys,
  When we were boys together!
When the grass was sweet to the bare brown feet
  That dimpled the laughing heather;

When the pewee sang to the summer dawn
  Of the bee in the billowy clover;
Or down by the mill the whippoorwill
  Echoed his night song over.

There is no love like the good old love,
  The love that mother gave us!
We are old, old men, yet we pine again
  For that precious grace—God save us!
So we dream and dream of the good old times,
  And our hearts grow tenderer, fonder,
As those dear old dreams bring soothing gleams
  Of Heaven away off yonder.

—Eugene Field.

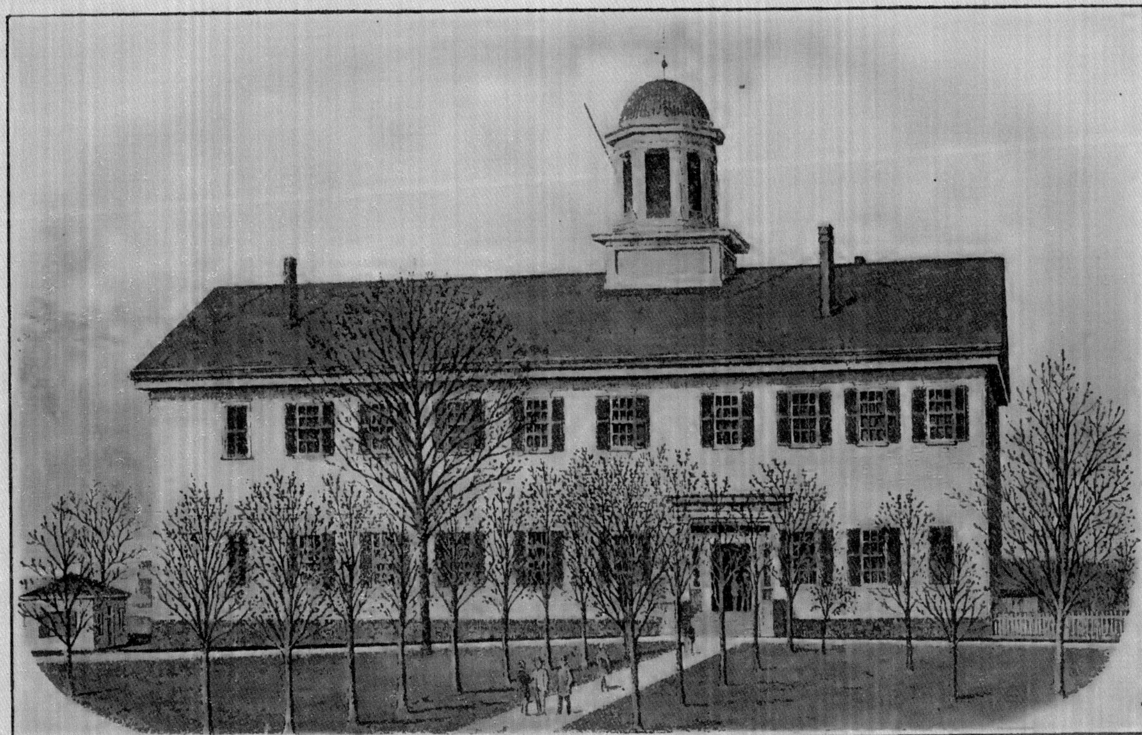

OLD CAPITOL BUILT IN 1847

RELATIVE TO PROFANITY.

Manner in Which Rev. Dow of New York Recovered An Axe.

Profanity in the abstract is quite bad enough, but pernicious and unintelligible, and I may say ill-directed profanity is simply a waste of time-honored expletives. I can remember very distinctly the first time I ever heard my father swear. We were then living near the little town of Shelby, N. Y., and father was presiding elder in the Christian church. The regular circuit rider for that territory had been taken suddenly sick and so father had to do the preaching at the Stapleton schoolhouse or get some one to do it. There was no time to look around, for Dad only received his notice about early candle-light Saturday night. So the old gent was stuck for the job all right. Hence the following morning, tolerable early, my big brother went out to the hovel with father to help hook on.

Now the day previous, father had traded horses with a friend from Lockport, and got boot, of course. However, the new equine acquisition was much longer than "Doll" and the traces must be "let out" a few holes, which was no easy thing to do, it would appear. However, father, being somewhat nervous and anxious for an early start, nearly broke his thumb trying to unbuckle the old stiff tug. Well, then came the expletives, not, of course, as classic and regular as they would be from a canal driver, but pretty good considering the want of practice.

Suffice it to say that Dad and Hank finally got things together and drove round to the cabin door. Hank helped mother into the sleigh and away they went and were soon out of sight in the woods. I used to like to see father in his Sunday clothes with his silk hat, swallow tailed coat, stand-up collar and wide, stiff, black dickey. Preach? Of course he could. But you should have heard mother tell of that particular "Sabbath day's journey." Of course, as was customary in those primitive days, the upper story or crown of a plug hat was a receptacle for any valuable papers or documents. At this particular time, father had his best sermon, together with sundry memorandums, receipts, dunning letters, etc., safely protected with a silk bandana 'kerchief.

Well, the wind was blowing as this pious couple pulled out, and it kept rising until it became almost a hurricane, and just as the elder was crossing a swiftly running way-side brook, only partially frozen over, Dad's hat blew off and into the stream, sermon and all. And it was a grand sermon too, one of Lorenzo Dow's best. And if good old Lorenzo had been there, he could have gathered up material for several, just as good, from among the solid, though somewhat disjointed hit-or-miss profanity that rattled along down that innocent brooklet, with here and there a water-soaked scrap of Dad's pet sermon.

Mr. Dow was an eccentric pioneer preacher and backwoodsman, of western New York, back in the early forties, and who has not heard of the fearless, rough-shod and unique Lorenzo Dow? It reminds me of some of the stories current in those days and undoubtedly true. I have heard my mother speak of him many times, as she was personally acquainted with this celebrated character. On one occasion where he was to hold forth in a log schoolhouse in the neighborhood, he was made acquainted with the fact that a certain infidel, who had lately moved into the settlement, intended to wage war with Lorenzo, and break up the meeting, and sure enough his Satanic majesty was there ready for the fray, and Mr. Dow had no sooner stepped behind the desk than our friend, the enemy, began to be noisy. However, the good minister started up in the usual manner, by invocation, taking apparently no heed to the disturbing element until he had given out the morning hymn when he remarked: "We will sing this hymn as soon as I convert this son of Belial." Suiting the action to the word, Lorenzo walked over to this stranger and began to talk with him. But the fellow was there for a purpose, and that purpose was to break up Mr. Dow's meeting. He therefore not only refused to desist but evinced a very lively willingness to fight.

"All right," says the elder. And pulling off his coat, he threw it on to the next desk, saying: "Lie there religion, until I flog this man." And he flogged that man, good and plenty, pounded him until he solemnly promised to be good, here and hereafter. And Mr. Dow then proceeded with the meeting as though nothing had happened.

On another occasion Rev. Mr. Dow rode into the settlement, as was his custom, late Saturday afternoon, preparatory to holding services on the following Sabbath. He put up at the home of Brother Patterson. As soon as convenient after supper, Brother Patterson unfolded the sorrowful misfortune of the loss of his axe while home at dinner and on returning to the woods his axe was gone. The elder bid him not to worry about it. Perhaps he could help him find it, he said. On the way to the school house next morning Mr. Dow picked up a good sized rock and carried it into church with him, laying it on the desk. After the invocation, the minister, a large and powerful man, straightened up to his full height and raising the rock as if to throw it, said: "I'm going to hit the man that stole Brother Patterson's axe."

One man dodged. Lorenzo looked over at Brother Patterson and coolly remarked: "Brother Patterson, Brother Jones has your axe." And right here comes up that same old proposition of profanity. Brother Patterson swore out a warrant for Brother Jones. Brother Jones swore he knew nothing of Brother Patterson's axe, and when the axe was found at Brother Jones' house, Brother Patterson proceeded to swear to the identity of the axe, so it seems to be a question as to whether we shall "swear not at all," unnecessarily, or whether it would be better simply to affirm. Of course circumstances and conditions always must be taken into consideration, and yet here we have an incompatibility, for no gentleman will use profanity and, vice versa, no habitually profane man can claim to be a gentleman, according to the rules and usages of clean, first-class society ethics.

MAPLE SUGAR MAKING.

Boiling Works Were Located at Corner of Capitol Avenue and Saginaw Street.

Pure maple sugar is a luxury. Our folks used to make it right here in the present corporate limits of the city 64 years ago. Our boiling works were located where now is the corner of Capitol avenue and Saginaw street and the "bush" comprised the adjacent region. We were novices in the business and father began by tapping any and all the larger trees. But an old woodman soon set us right and the several children of us went to work gathering sap. Our largest and most productive tree stood on the spot where Bailey Buck now lives. Near this tree was a large grape vine on which we youngsters were wont to swing. I shall never forget what one of these swings cost me. I had tarried too long at the vine and as a punishment father elected that I should keep my eldest brother company at the "boiling down" that night. Everything was serene until near midnight. I was sitting half asleep under a large tree near the fire when I was fairly raised from the ground by a most unearthly shriek. My big brother solemnly assured me that the noise came from the "prince of darkness" in the top of that tree and that he was undoubtedly after me, and I momentarily expected to see Old Nick himself sliding down that basswood and landing at my very feet.

I had battled with every known species of reptile on the school section. I had sat in the twilight on a log and listened complacently to the plaintive cry of the wily panther. I had seized the young cub by the tail and run homeward with it just to vex the mother bear and make her show her teeth. I had sat with my brothers and sisters on the cabin floor inside the open door and tossed chips at the growling wolf. But I was glad enough when we finally returned to the cabin. I was soon in bed and covered up head and ears. I went to sleep, but oh, what dreams.

I saw his Satanic Majesty come up the ladder, and with a hellish grin on his smooty face he made straight for me, and gathering me up he soared away into the inky space that lay between our peaceful cabin and his far famed abode, to say I was frightened would be too weak an expression altogether, I tried the power of prayer. I could only think of the oft-repeated prayer my mother taught me to say on retiring, "now I lay me down to sleep," etc., but this would not do on an occasion of this kind, however. On we sped, the great black wings sending us on through space at a rapid pace and only when I began to feel the fervent heat and smell the fumes of sulphur did I awake to the realization that, very fortunately for me, it was only a horrid dream. I learned on the following day that the cause of all my misery was simply a harmless screech owl. I had never heard one of these birds sing before. I have heard similar sounds since, at the "morning service."

I remember one beautiful Sabbath morning in the summer of 1851, just after prayers. Father had no sooner said amen when a neighbor bolted in the open door and yelled, "Hogs in your garden, Bro. Mevis." Dad flew for the garden and over the fence like a colt. Seizing a fence stake in his flight he went after those hogs and undertook to drive them back into the sty, but they ran in every direction but the right one. Mother saw what a hard time he was having and how blue the air was getting around father and she caught up the swill pail, filled it at the barrel and slipped out to the pen and quietly called, pig, pig, pig, and every hog came to her as fast as they could get there, and into the pen they went. A practical demonstration of the power of moral suasion vs. brute force.

SELAH.